5/05

W9-CBR-387

Ethiopia

Ethiopia

BY ANN HEINRICHS

Enchantment of the World
Second Series

Children's Press®

A Division of Scholastic Inc.

NEW YORK   TORONTO   LONDON   AUCKLAND   SYDNEY
MEXICO CITY   NEW DELHI   HONG KONG
DANBURY, CONNECTICUT

Frontispiece: A group of young goat herders rests on a hillside in Arba Minch, Ethiopia

Consultant: Shimelis Bonsa, Ph.D. candidate, Department of History, University of California–Los Angeles; former lecturer in history, Addis Ababa University, Addis Ababa, Ethiopia

Please note: All statistics are as up-to-date as possible at the time of publication.

Book production by Herman Adler Design

Library of Congress Cataloging-in-Publication Data

Heinrichs, Ann.
  Ethiopia / by Ann Heinrichs.
        p. cm. — (Enchantment of the world. Second series)
  Includes bibliographical references and index.
  ISBN 0-516-23680-6
  1. Ethiopia—Juvenile literature. I. Title. II. Series.
    DT373.H45 2005
    963—dc22   2004016194

Acknowledgments

The author is most grateful to Yohannes Assefa of Red Jackal Tours for his sensitive and knowledgable guidance and for his many insights into Ethiopian culture; to Tsegaye Tirfe for his guidance through northern Ethiopia; to Irma Turtle of Turtle Tours and Turtle Will; and to the many people of Ethiopia who shared their wisdom and hospitality.

Cover photo:
Young Hamer girl

Contents

CHAPTER

Blue Nile Falls

Young Amhara shepherd

Ancient Kingdoms, Rich Traditions

8

It is early morning, and Aikey leads his herd of cattle past rocks and thorny bushes. At a dry riverbed he digs deep into the sand until a trickle of water appears. Digging deeper, he brings up pans of water and pours them into a trough for his thirsty cattle.

At the same time Adanech puts on her bright green uniform before the long walk to school. She hopes to pass the national exams and fulfill her dream of going to college. Meanwhile, Abebe has been beating the drum for hours. It is the feast of his church's patron saint, and he is marking time as the priests recite their chants.

All these children are Ethiopians. Their ways of life are very different, yet each one paints an image of Ethiopia's diverse culture. Ethiopia is one of the oldest nations on Earth. This land of ancient kingdoms was known as Abyssinia for much of its history. From high atop their mountain fortresses, mighty kings and princes ruled lands far beyond the nation's present-day borders.

Ethiopia's religious history is very much a part of its national pride. Its centuries-long line of emperors claimed to have roots in biblical times. Today's Ethiopian

Opposite: **Throughout Ethiopia, children live different lifestyles. They may be cattle herders, farmers, or students.**

Centuries ago, Ethiopia was ruled by kings and emperors.

Ethiopia has a rich religious heritage based on centuries-old traditions.

Ethiopia's many ethnic groups take great pride in their country's culture and traditions.

Orthodox Church treasures its ancient heritage. In the city of Axum, according to tradition, rests the Ark of the Covenant—the chest containing the tablets of the Ten Commandments. The religion of Islam thrives in Ethiopia, too. The city of Harer is a holy place for the Islamic world.

Among African nations Ethiopia holds a place of honor. Except for a five-year period, it is the only African country that never became a European colony. Ethiopia is also Africa's oldest independent nation. The colors of its flag—green, yellow, and red—are known as the pan-African colors because they were adopted by so many other African countries.

Many outsiders hear of Ethiopia only as a place of drought, famine, and wars. Civil wars wracked the country in the 1980s, and border conflicts continued for years. At the same time Ethiopia suffered a devastating drought. Crop failures left more than one million people dead. Poverty and hunger are still serious problems, as most Ethiopians depend on farming to make a living. They rely on rains that may or may not fall.

This picture is far from complete, though. The sheer beauty of Ethiopia would surprise anyone who has never seen it. Much of the land is lush and green, with tropical forests, fertile valleys, terraced hillsides, and grassy plains. Rugged mountain peaks overlook sparkling lakes and spectacular gorges. Up in the highlands is the Blue Nile Falls, an immense torrent of water crashing down into the canyon below.

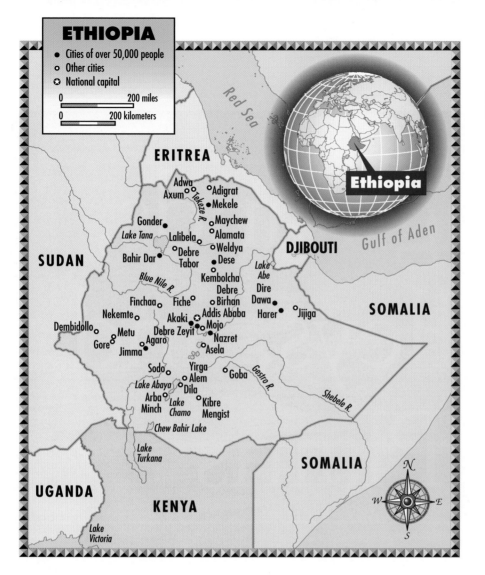

Geopolitical map of Ethiopia

Alongside all this natural beauty is a rich and vibrant culture that hardships cannot crush. Ethiopia is home to dozens of ethnic groups. Though they are very different, most live side by side in mutual respect. Each group is proud of its centuries-old traditions. These traditions give dignity and meaning to everyday life. In a world of conflicts and shifting values, Ethiopia offers lessons for us all.

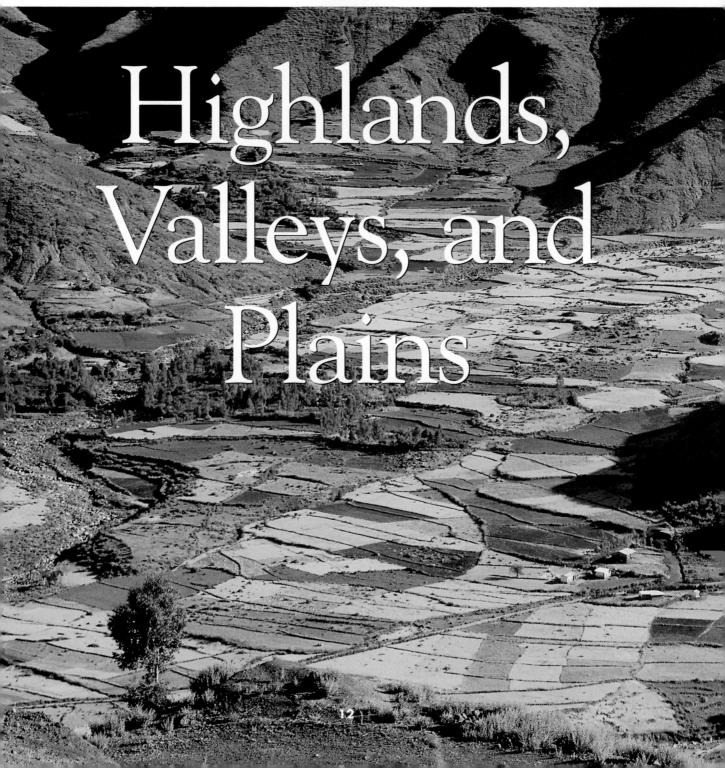

Highlands, Valleys, and Plains

ETHIOPIA IS A RUGGED AND BEAUTIFUL LAND WITH HIGH rocky mountains and flat-topped plateaus. Deep gorges and river valleys cut through the highlands, and sparkling lakes nestle among the hills. Across the lowlands, rolling plains and grasslands stretch as far as the eye can see.

Ethiopia is a nation in northeast Africa. It is located on a piece of land called the Horn of Africa. Ethiopian kings once ruled the entire Horn. In those times, Ethiopia faced the Arabian Peninsula across the Red Sea. Many cultural ties connected Ethiopia with Arabia.

Today, Ethiopia is the tenth-largest of the fifty-three African nations. It is almost twice the size of the state of Texas and almost three times the size of California. To the north is Eritrea. Djibouti and Somalia lie to the east. Sudan is on the west, and Kenya borders the south. Ethiopia's southern border is less than 250 miles (402 kilometers) north of the equator.

The Great Rift Valley

Volcanoes and earthquakes have made Ethiopia's surface very uneven over time. The largest "crack" is the Great Rift Valley, which runs through Ethiopia from north to south. This valley is a deep groove in Earth's crust. It stretches for thousands of miles, from the Jordan River valley in Syria to Mozambique in southeastern Africa.

The northern part of the Great Rift Valley is called the Danakil Plain, or the Danakil Desert. Within this arid lowland is the Danakil Depression, Ethiopia's lowest point and the hottest place on Earth. The Danakil Plain was once an inland sea. Its waters evaporated, leaving rich deposits of salt behind.

Farther south, the Rift Valley turns into a green and fertile countryside, flourishing with tropical woodlands. A chain of beautiful lakes runs through this region. Many hot springs are found there, too.

Highlands and Lowlands

At one time, the Danakil Plain was a great inland sea. Today, vast amounts of salt deposits remain there.

About two-thirds of Ethiopia's land is on the Ethiopian Plateau. On it lies the country's best farmland and its biggest cities. The Great Rift Valley cuts through the plateau, separating the western highlands from the eastern highlands. These highlands slope down to the dry lowlands of the east, west, and south.

A small village on Ethiopia's central plateau

Ethiopia's western highlands are often called the central and northern plateaus. They consist of steep-sided mountains with deep gorges between them and flat-topped peaks called *ambas*. These high places once made natural fortresses for Ethiopia's kings, whose capital cities looked down from the heights. Axum, Gondar (also Gonder), and Lalibela were capitals of great kingdoms in past centuries. Addis Ababa, high on the central plateau, is now Ethiopia's capital.

Lalibela

The town of Lalibela is named after King Lalibela of the Zagwe dynasty. When he was an infant, his mother saw bees swarming around him. Believing that creatures can sense important people, she named him Lalibela, which means "bees recognize his sovereignty."

Lalibela built his capital city high on a plateau. Deeply religious, he saw this place as a "new Jerusalem." He even named the city's stream the Jordan, after the Holy Land's Jordan River. During his reign (1185–1225), Lalibela had eleven churches carved into solid tufa (left), the pinkish-red volcanic rock that makes up the plateau. Today these churches are pilgrimage sites for thousands of Ethiopian Orthodox Christians.

The Simien Mountains, on the northern plateau, are Ethiopia's highest mountain range. Many peaks in the Simien Range rise over 13,000 feet (3,962 meters) high. Among them is Ras Dejen, or Ras Dashen. It is the highest point in Ethiopia and the fourth-tallest mountain in Africa. Far below, the western lowlands run along Ethiopia's western border with Sudan and continue into the southwest.

The eastern highlands cover a smaller area than the western highlands. There, the mountains run in a narrow band alongside the Rift Valley. The major cities are Dire Dawa and Harer. The Ogaden is an arid plain stretching from the eastern highlands to the Somalian border. It is sparsely populated and has no large towns.

Ethiopia's Geographic Features

Area: 435,184 square miles (1,127,127 sq km)

Highest Elevation: Ras Dejen (Ras Dashen), 15,158 feet (4,620 m) above sea level

Lowest Elevation: Danakil Depression, 410 feet (125 m) below sea level

Largest Lake: Lake Tana, about 1,400 square miles (3,626 sq km)

Major Rivers: Blue Nile (Abay), Omo, Awash, and Wabe Shebele

Greatest Distance North to South: 800 miles (1,287 km)

Greatest Distance East to West: 1,035 miles (1,665 km)

Highest Annual Rainfall: Up to 80 inches (203 cm) in the southwestern highlands

Lowest Annual Rainfall: 0–20 inches (0–51 cm) in the Danakil Plain

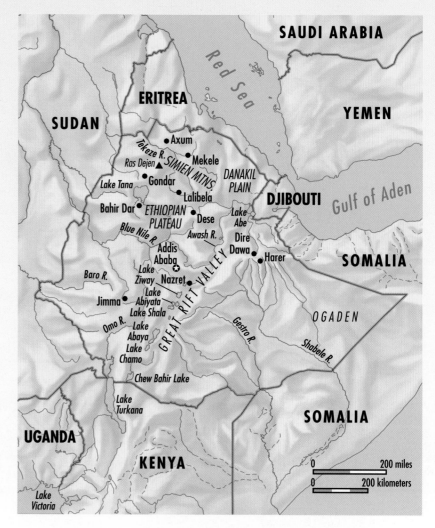

Average Temperature, Highlands: 62°F (17°C)
Average Temperature, Lowlands: 82°F (28°C)

Lakes

Lake Tana is Ethiopia's largest lake. It lies in the northern highlands between Gondar and Bahir Dar. Many rivers flow from the lake, providing irrigation for crops in some parts of the country. Gliding along the lake are *tankwas*, or papyrus canoes, loaded with firewood and vegetables for market. Thirty-seven islands are scattered across the lake. On many of them are churches and monasteries that were built hundreds of years ago.

Many sparkling lakes lie along the Rift Valley. From north to south, they include Lakes Ziway, Langano, Abiyata, Shala, Abaya, and Chamo. They are popular spots for vacationers and wildlife watchers. Lake Turkana, once called Lake Rudolf, crosses the southern border into Kenya. Lake Chew Bahir, once Lake Stephanie, is another southern lake.

A papyrus canoe glides along Lake Tana, Ethiopia's largest lake.

The Blue Nile River, Ethiopia's major river.

Rivers

Ethiopia's rivers rise in the highlands and flow down in many directions. The largest and best-known Ethiopian river is the Blue Nile, called Abay in Ethiopia's Amharic language. It joins the White Nile near Khartoum in neighboring Sudan. Once joined, they form the Nile River, the longest river in the world. About 86 percent of the Nile's waters come from the Blue Nile.

The Blue Nile rises from a spring near Lake Tana and flows through a channel in the lake. Soon after it emerges, the river cascades down as the Blue Nile Falls. It continues through the Blue Nile Gorge, tracing a great curve on its way to Sudan. The Blue Nile generates much of the north's hydroelectric power.

The Tekeze and Baro rivers also run through the northern highlands. In the southeast the Shabele is the major river. It rises in Ethiopia and flows into Somalia. The Omo River is the major waterway in the southwest. It winds through the region, sometimes swirling through rapids, on its way to Lake Turkana. The Awash River rises in the central highlands and comes to an end on the Danakil Plain.

The Blue Nile Falls

One of Africa's most spectacular waterfalls is the Blue Nile Falls. It drops over a sheer cliff of basalt rock, crashing more than 150 feet (46 m) below. Ethiopians call the falls Tissisat, meaning "smoke of fire." Its waters create a misty, smokelike spray that catches rainbows in the sunlight.

Climate

Ethiopia is sometimes called the land of eternal spring. Throughout much of the country, visitors can enjoy springtime weather almost any time of year.

Ethiopia is located in the tropics—the band around Earth that lies close to the equator. However, its climate depends on the elevation of the land. The highlands range from warm to cool, but the highest regions can get quite cold. Temperatures in the lowlands are generally high. The hottest area is the Danakil desert, where temperatures may rise as high as 120 degrees Fahrenheit (49 degrees Celsius).

The Danakil desert is Ethiopia's hottest region, with temperatures reaching as high as 120°F.

A huge storm cloud approaches Bale Mountains National Park.

Ethiopia's main seasonal differences are wet and dry. The rainy season comes in two segments that are very close to each other. The *belg*—the "little rains," or spring rains—begin in late February or early March and last through April. After a short dry spell come the heavy summer rains. They are the *keremt*, or "big rains," which last from mid-May or June through September. After that comes a long dry season.

These dry and wet cycles vary somewhat from one region to another. For example, some parts of the western highlands may get rain all year long. On the other extreme, there are years when the Danakil Plain gets no rain at all.

The rains vary from year to year, too. Sometimes the belg rains arrive late or fail to come at all. This creates a problem for farmers who raise belg-season crops. In some years there may not be much of a gap between the two rainy seasons. Then the ground becomes waterlogged or even flooded. Both these conditions can result in serious food shortages.

Traditional Regions

Ethiopia was divided into nine states in 1995. (See chapter 5.) Before that, the country was made up of smaller regional units that were divided along cultural and historical lines.

Ethiopians still often use the names of traditional regions and provinces when they refer to an area. Wollo, Kaffa, and Sidamo, for example, are names of traditional regions.

Looking at Ethiopia's Cities

Dire Dawa in eastern Ethiopia began in 1902 as a terminal for the Addis Ababa–Djibouti railway. Now it is a major trade center and Ethiopia's second-largest city. Along its tree-lined streets are many buildings in both Arabic and European styles. The colorful Kefira market draws camel trains from the desert, as well as local people wearing traditional clothing.

Nazret, south of Addis Ababa, was named for Jesus's childhood home of Nazareth. It is the country's third-largest city and a center for commerce and small-scale industries. Nazret is also a trade center for the area's farmers, plantation owners, and cattle herders.

Gondar stands high in the mountains north of Lake Tana. It was founded by Emperor Fasilidas in 1636 and remained Ethiopia's capital for more than two hundred years. Within Fasilidas's royal compound (above)

are castles, banquet halls, stables, and an outdoor bathing pool. Nearby is the Empress Mintwab's castle compound. Gondar's Debre Berhan Selassie Church is known for the dozens of angels painted on its ceiling.

Dese is the capital of the Wollo region. It lies at the foot of Mount Tossa, midway between the central plateau and the Great Rift Valley. Some say Dese's name comes from the language of the Oromo people. Others say Ethiopian Emperor Yohannes IV gave the city its name, which means "my joy" in Amharic. Dese is a crossroads for travel and trade between Addis Ababa and northeastern Ethiopia.

Mekele is the capital of Tigray, Ethiopia's northernmost regional state. Overlooking the Danakil Plain, it is a center for Ethiopia's salt trade. Camels arrive in the market laden with blocks of salt. Yohannes IV made

Mekele his capital in the late 1800s, and a local museum displays artifacts from his reign.

Bahir Dar, on the southern shore of Lake Tana, is the capital of Amhara regional state. It is a busy city, with many offices and shops located along its tree-lined streets. For visitors, Bahir Dar is a base for visiting the Blue Nile Falls and Lake Tana's island monasteries.

Jimma is the largest city in western Ethiopia. It was once the capital city of powerful Oromo kings. Today it is the trade center for the coffee-growing southwest region. Jimma is also known for its fine woodworkers, who make three-legged stools and other furniture.

Harer is a historic walled city in eastern Ethiopia. Founded in the seventh century A.D., it was built into a Muslim stronghold in the 1520s. With more than ninety mosques, it is a holy city and pilgrimage site for Muslims. The old city walls still stand, and the streets are lined with traditional Hareri houses.

Axum was the seat of Ethiopia's Axumite kingdom, which became Ethiopia's dominant power in the first century A.D. (see chapter 4). It is known for its ancient stone pillars (right), Saint Mary of Zion Church, and the nearby chapel of the Ark of the Covenant.

Lalibela is famous for its eleven churches carved out of solid rock. They were built by the twelfth-century king Lalibela (see sidebar on page 16).

Ethiopia in the Wild

F

RISKY MONKEYS AND BABOONS SWING THROUGH THE branches and scamper across the fields. At night their screeches and barks pierce the air. Ethiopia is teeming with wildlife. While some animals are shy or hard to spot, others are hard to miss!

Black and white colobus monkeys leap from one tree to another. They are quite a sight as they sail through the air, for their long tails have a fluffy white plume on the end. Colobus monkeys used to be hunted for their silky fur, but they are now protected. Packs of baboons range through the countryside and can be troublesome pests. They raid farmers' fields and munch on grains and vegetables, quickly destroying the season's crops.

Jackals and hyenas roam throughout much of Ethiopia. These crafty hunters are the subjects of many folktales. They howl and cry when they hunt at night, making a hair-raising racket.

Many kinds of antelope inhabit the lowlands. They include the oryx, the kudu, and the waterbuck. The tiny dik-dik weighs only about 10 pounds (4.5 kilograms). This shrub-eating antelope is named for the sound it

Opposite: **Colobus monkeys are just one of a variety of animals that make their home in Ethiopia.**

A jackal stops for a drink of water.

Three gerenuks feast on the tender leaves of this tree.

makes when it is scared. The gerenuk is a long-legged, long-necked antelope. It stands on its hind legs and props its front legs against tree trunks to nibble the leaves.

Hippopotamuses and crocodiles live along the riverbanks and lakeshores. One spot on Lake Chamo is known as the "crocodile market." Hundreds of crocs gather there to cool off in the water or bask in the sun.

Birds, Bees, and Termites

More than eight hundred bird species live in Ethiopia. Plump, strong-legged guinea fowl skitter across the ground while vultures, eagles, hawks, and falcons soar overhead. Thousands of waterbirds nest by the Rift Valley lakes. There you will find pelicans, kingfishers, ibises, herons, flamingos, and marabou storks. Across the lowlands, trees are clustered with weaverbird nests. They look like round, grassy baskets hanging from the branches.

A marabou stork approaches a good resting place in a marsh.

Weaverbirds build nests that dangle from tree branches.

Many of Ethiopia's birds come in brilliant colors. One is the carmine bee-eater, with plumage in dazzling shades of red and blue. Another is the Abyssinian roller, with its striking turquoise plumage. Other birds have bizarre bills, such as the thick-billed raven and the Abyssinian ground hornbill.

Birds are not the only creatures that nest in the trees. Many trees are bristling with beehives—long barrels made of bamboo or straw. The bees are prized for their honey, a valuable product in Ethiopia.

Bee-eaters brighten the Ethiopian landscape with their vivid reds and blues.

Termite nests are an awesome sight. Their tall, reddish towers dominate the landscape in the dry lowlands. Birds perch high on the towers as lookouts, and some birds make holes in the mounds for their own nests. Jackals and mongooses often make their dens in the mounds, too.

In the dry lowlands, termites sometimes build mounds that almost reach the treetops!

Rare and Endangered Animals

Trek into the bush in the early morning, listen carefully, and you may hear the distant roar of a lion. Ethiopia used to have lots of large wild animals. Lions, leopards, giraffes, elephants, and rhinoceroses once thrived in the grasslands and forests. Unfortunately, big-game hunters have almost wiped them out. Now it is illegal to hunt these animals, and the government is cracking down hard on poachers, or illegal hunters. Some large animals still inhabit the Rift Valley, the Omo River valley, and the western lowlands. Among them are warthogs, wild buffalo, and Swayne's hartebeest.

Warthogs are often seen in Ethiopia's dry grasslands.

An Ethiopian wolf mother with her pups in Bale Mountains National Park.

Some animals in Ethiopia are not found anywhere else in the world. Because their populations are so small, they are classified as rare, threatened, or endangered.

The elegant, long-legged Ethiopian wolf goes by many other names—Simien fox, Simien jackal, Abyssinian jackal, and red jackal, or *ky kebero* in Amharic. It is the world's rarest dog species, with only a few hundred remaining. Most live in Bale Mountains National Park, with scattered packs in the Simien Mountains and other highland regions.

The endangered walia ibex is a sturdy wild goat that scrambles among the rocky slopes of the Simien Mountains. Another endangered species is the mountain nyala, a slender antelope with long, curved horns. It is found only in the mountains near Lake Ziway.

The gelada is a large baboon with a big mane of golden hair around its face. Sometimes called the lion baboon, it is found only in the high meadows and forests of the northern highlands. The gelada grazes on grass and leaves. It uses its long, sharp fangs for fighting enemies.

A male gelada baboon (center) has a lionlike mane of hair.

Protected Areas

Ethiopia has set aside dozens of national parks, wildlife sanctuaries, and game preserves to protect disappearing species and let their populations increase. Two of the parks—Simien

The Walia Ibex

The walia ibex is one of Ethiopia's most endangered animals. This nimble goat lives only in Simien Mountains National Park. In the late 1990s, fewer than two hundred animals remained. The ibex dwells on steep cliffs and rocky mountain outcrops. It becomes active in the evening and early morning, feeding on bushes, grasses, and herbs.

The walia ibex used to be fairly safe from hunters because its habitat was so hard to reach. Since hunters began using modern firearms in the 1920s, however, its population has declined.

Walia ibexes are among the many rare animals that are found in Simien Mountains National Park. Thus, the park is listed as a World Heritage in Danger Site by the United Nations Educational, Scientific, and Cultural Organization (UNESCO).

Simien Mountains National Park is one of several protected areas within Ethiopia.

Mountains and Bale Mountains national parks—are in the highlands. Besides preserving many rare animals, they offer breathtaking mountain scenery. Several parks surround the Rift Valley lakes, where birdwatchers love to roam.

In the southwest, Mago and Omo national parks lie alongside the Omo River. Mago National Park preserves wildlife across broad stretches of savannah. Omo National Park is not often visited because it is so hard to reach. This vast wilderness is known for its wildlife as well as its white-water rapids. Awash National Park lies east of Addis Ababa. It surrounds the Awash River, whose falls tumble into a spectacular gorge.

Trees, Flowers, and Grasses

Ethiopia's plant life is as varied as its landscape and climate. Evergreens such as cedar and juniper grow on the high mountainsides. Where rainfall is plentiful, there may be dense

The Meskal Daisy

The Meskal daisy blankets Ethiopia's fields and hillsides in September, turning them into a shimmering sea of gold. The daisy is beloved both for its beauty and for its place in the year's cycle of celebrations. It brings a joyful welcome to the New Year, which begins on September 11 in Ethiopia. However, it is named for the Ethiopian Orthodox feast of Meskal, the Feast of the True Cross, which falls on September 27.

tropical forests with thick underbrush. Eucalyptus trees were introduced into Ethiopia in the 1890s. Today, they're found throughout much of the country.

Flowering plants create surprising splashes of orange, red, purple, pink, and gold. The bright red poinsettia, a traditional Christmas flower in North America, grows as a tree in Ethiopia. Jacaranda trees, clustered with purple blossoms, beautify many cities and towns. Even the high mountain meadows are dotted with colorful wildflowers.

Aloe plants grow in Ethiopia's lowlands.

Tough, hardy plants that can stand heat and long dry spells are found in the dry lowlands. One is the aloe, called *erret* in Amharic. Its plump leaves store moisture and are sometimes used as a medicine. Cactuses also grow throughout the countryside. Some people plant cactuses as a fence around their homes and fields. This is a good way to keep livestock in and wild animals out.

A donkey rests in the shade of a tree in one of Ethiopia's many regions where trees are few and far between.

Savannah, or dry grassland, covers much of the lowlands. Trees are scattered here and there above the tall, golden grasses. The most common savannah trees are acacias. Their long roots reach water far underground. One type is called umbrella acacia because its branches spread out wide at the top. Although acacias bear long thorns, their leaves are tasty forage for antelopes, camels, and other animals.

Herbal Medicines

For centuries Ethiopians have used wild herbs as medicines. Herbal healers use various plants to treat ailments such as malaria, hepatitis, pneumonia, and even tapeworms.

Many ethnic groups are known for their familiarity with medicinal plants. They include the Anuak of the western lowlands and the Boro of the northwest.

Scientists in Ethiopia are studying many of these herbal remedies to see if they may be useful in developing new drugs. Scientists point out that common western drugs such as aspirin and morphine were derived from traditional folk medicines.

The Birthplace of Coffee

Most of the world's coffee today is made from beans of the arabica coffee plant, *Coffea arabica*. This plant originated in Ethiopia's highlands, where it has been growing wild for more than two thousand years.

Coffee (*bunna* in Amharic) grows wild throughout much of Ethiopia. Most coffee, though, is cultivated in the southern and western highlands, where the altitude and plentiful rainfall are ideal for its growth. Coffee trees abound in the wild forests of the Kaffa region. In fact, it is believed that the Kaffa region gave coffee its name. The Sidamo, Gamo-Gofa, and Welega regions are also rich coffee producers.

An Ethiopian coffee farmer picks coffee beans on his farm.

From Ethiopia, coffee was introduced to present-day Yemen, on the Arabian Peninsula. Yemeni traders spread coffee throughout Arabia, and it soon reached the rest of the Muslim world. European traders discovered this exotic drink in the 1500s and took it to Europe. Many countries produce coffee now, but coffee lovers swear that Ethiopian coffee is the best!

CHAPTER

FOUR

Kingdoms, Princes, and the Modern Nation

E THIOPIA HOLDS MANY TREASURES FOR anthropologists. These scientists study human beings and their ancestors. Each discovery is another piece of the great puzzle about human origins.

In 1974, anthropologists were digging in the Hadar region in northeastern Ethiopia. They uncovered the partial skeleton of a young woman. She was about twenty years old, 3 feet 6 inches (1.07 m) tall, and weighed around 60 pounds (27 kilograms). They gave her the scientific name *Australopithecus afarensis*. Feeling that she deserved a more personal name, they called her Lucy.

At the time of discovery, Lucy and her relatives were the earliest human ancestors ever found. They were more than 3 million years old. They walked upright and lived in groups, roaming the lush forests that then covered the region. Even older remains were found in Hadar in 2001. Dated at more than 5 million years old, they are the earliest known ancestors of modern humans.

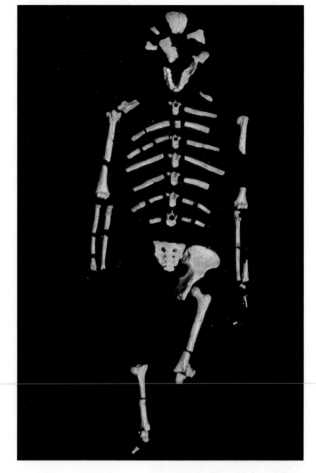

Lucy, one of humans' earliest ancestors, lived in Ethiopia more than 3 million years ago. Anthropologists found her remains in the Hadar region.

Early Ethiopians

By about 7000 B.C., people who spoke Omotic and Cushitic languages had settled in Ethiopia. Omotic speakers lived in

Opposite: **Emperor Menelik II is honored by this statue in Addis Ababa, Ethiopia's capital.**

Wonderful Lucy

Donald Johnson, leader of the team that found the Lucy skeleton, explains how she got her name. Shortly after the discovery, the archaeologists heard the Beatles song "Lucy in the Sky with Diamonds" on their camp radio. At once they decided on Lucy as the young woman's name. Ethiopians call her Dinqinesh, meaning "You Are Wonderful." A replica of the skeleton is on display at the National Museum in Addis Ababa.

the central and southern highlands, while Cushitic speakers made their homes in the north. These people raised teff, barley, and other grains and kept domestic animals, such as sheep, goats, and cattle. Their languages evolved into many of Ethiopia's modern languages.

As early as 3000 B.C., Egyptians were trading with Ethiopia, a land they called Punt. Ethiopia had an abundance of myrrh, an aromatic plant substance the Egyptians needed. They burned myrrh as an incense and used it to preserve the bodies of the dead.

Around 3000 B.C., Ethiopians began providing Egyptians with exotic trade goods.

Around 1000 B.C., people from Arabia began to migrate across the Red Sea to Ethiopia. They came mainly from the kingdom of Saba, or Sheba, in present-day Yemen. These people spoke a Semitic language that was the ancestor of Ethiopia's modern Amharic and Tigrinya languages. They also brought a writing system—Sabaean—which developed into Ethiopia's ancient Ge'ez script.

In the first three centuries B.C., Egypt was ruled by the Ptolemy dynasty. The Ptolemies were descendants of leaders of the ancient Greek empire of Alexander the Great. They established settlements in Ethiopia and introduced Greek culture and arts to the region.

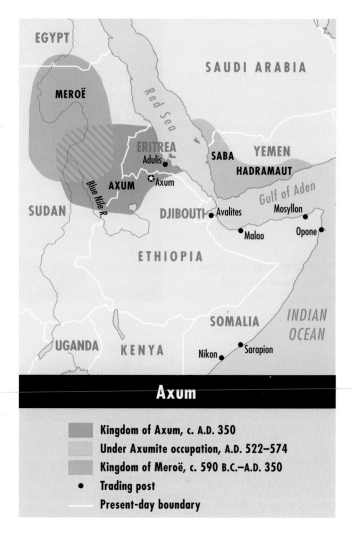

Axum

▨	**Kingdom of Axum, c. A.D. 350**
▨	**Under Axumite occupation, A.D. 522–574**
▨	**Kingdom of Meroë, c. 590 B.C.–A.D. 350**
•	**Trading post**
—	**Present-day boundary**

The Axumite Kingdom

Ethiopia's first great empire was the kingdom of Axum (sometimes spelled Aksum). It arose in the highlands of today's Tigray region and Eritrea in perhaps the second century B.C. Axum reached the height of its power from the A.D. 300s through the 500s.

Major Periods in Ethiopian History

Pre-Axumite period	Before second century B.C.
Axumite Kingdom	Flourished A.D. first through sixth centuries
Zagwe Dynasty	c. 1137–1270
Solomonid Dynasty	1270–1974
Reign of Haile Selassie	1930–1974
Rule of the Derg	1974–1991
Democratic Republic	1995–

A group of stelae, or stone pillars, stand in a field at Axum.

Axum, with its Red Sea port at Adulis, became the gateway for foreigners' trade with much of Africa. African gold, ivory, leather, incense, and spices all passed through Axum. The Axumites also developed trade and cultural ties with Egypt, the Greek Empire, and Arabia. Axum's merchants traded as far east as Persia, India, and even China. From time to time Axumite kings even ruled parts of the Arabian coast and Saba. They also came to rule regions to the west, in present-day Sudan. Axumite rulers called themselves *negusa nagast* ("king of kings"). The title signified that they ruled many regions that paid tribute to them.

The Axumites had a highly developed culture. They wrote in Greek, Sabaean, and Ge'ez scripts and built many stone palaces and monuments, especially in the capital city of Axum. Among the monuments of Axum are more than one hundred stone stelae, or pillars. These memorials to past kings are carved with inscriptions of each king's glorious deeds.

The arrival of Christianity was a major event in the Axumite period. Around A.D. 330, the Axumite king Ezana converted to Christianity and made it Axum's official religion. This marks the birth of today's Ethiopian Orthodox Church. The faith spread throughout the kingdom, and many religious communities called monasteries flourished in the years to come.

Hand-painted pictures in a very old religious text.

The Zagwe Dynasty

Axum gradually declined over the next centuries. In the 600s, the new religion of Islam began spreading across Arabia and beyond. By the mid-800s, Muslims, the followers of Islam, had converted many peoples living south and east of Ethiopia's highlands. Muslim traders also controlled Axum's old trade routes on the Red Sea.

Piece by piece, the Axumite kings lost control of their realm, and Ethiopia entered a period known as its dark ages. Meanwhile, the Axumites' well-developed culture still flourished in the highlands south of Axum. In the Lasta region a Christian kingdom ruled by the Zagwe dynasty came to power around 1137.

The Zagwe kings built new churches and monasteries and encouraged Christian literature and arts. The greatest of the

Zagwe kings was Lalibela. He had eleven churches cut out of solid rock at his capital of Roha. This city came to be called Lalibela in his honor.

The Solomonic Restoration

In time, leaders in other regions opposed the Zagwe. In 1270, an Amharic prince from the Shewa region named Yekuno Amlak overthrew the Zagwe regime and took the throne. He proclaimed that he was descended from King Solomon and the Queen of Sheba through their son, Menelik I. Yekuno Amlak thus established—or reestablished—the Solomonid dynasty, also called the Solomonic Restoration. This dynasty would rule Ethiopia for more than seven hundred years.

King Yekuno Amlak is known for proclaiming Ethiopia's Solomonid dynasty, which ruled for more than seven hundred years.

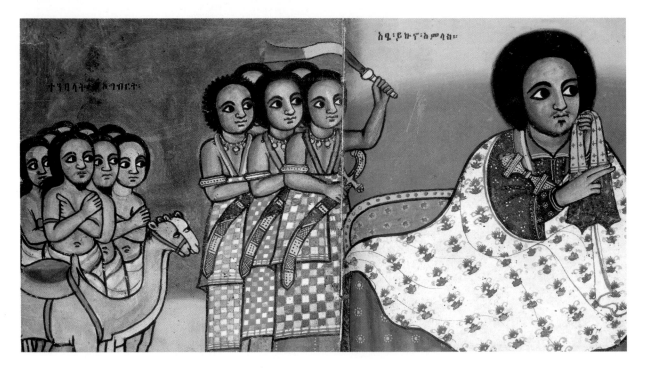

It was only a matter of time until Ethiopia had to deal with European powers. In the early 1500s, Portuguese navigators began exploring and trading along the Red Sea. They found the coast controlled by traders from the Muslim Ottoman Empire. Portugal began sending representatives to Ethiopia, with whom it had a common enemy. Soon a Muslim leader named Ahmad Grañ (Ahmed the Left-Handed) began waging war against Christian Ethiopia. With the help of Ottoman guns, he led his conquest through the central and northern highlands. In 1541, the Portuguese sent troops to help Ethiopia battle Ahmad Grañ. The Christian forces were able to take back much of Ethiopia for the time being.

Meanwhile, a new group of people was arriving from the south. The Oromo people inhabited what is now southern Ethiopia and northern Kenya. In the 1500s, they began migrating northward, spreading across the lowlands and reaching deeply into the highlands. The Oromo, who had their own native religion, pushed the Christian empire back to the northern and central districts.

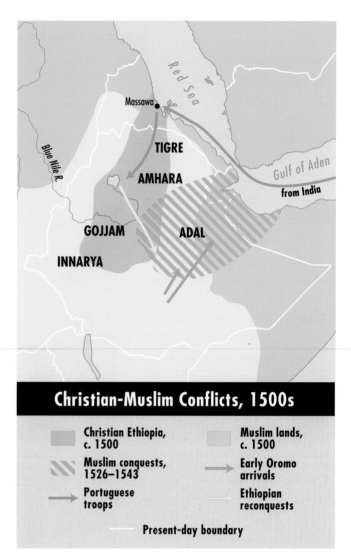

Christian-Muslim Conflicts, 1500s

- Christian Ethiopia, c. 1500
- Muslim conquests, 1526–1543
- Portuguese troops
- Muslim lands, c. 1500
- Early Oromo arrivals
- Ethiopian reconquests
- Present-day boundary

Solomon, Makeda, and Menelik

The Queen of Sheba, known in Ethiopia as Makeda, is an important figure in Ethiopian tradition. The Bible's Old Testament tells of the queen's meeting with Solomon, king of the Israelites. Ethiopia's national epic, *Kebra Negast (The Glory of Kings)*, adds many details drawn from Ethiopian tradition. These details add a rich spiritual texture to Ethiopia's history. They also place the roots of the emperors' authority firmly in biblical times.

According to the *Kebra Negast*, Makeda was an Ethiopian queen who traveled to Jerusalem to visit the great King Solomon (right). Makeda conceived a son by Solomon, returned to Ethiopia, and gave birth to Menelik I.

When he grew up, Menelik journeyed to Jerusalem to see his father. Solomon recognized Menelik and rejoiced in meeting his first-born son. When Menelik left for Ethiopia, he took with him the Ark of the Covenant. This was the ornate chest containing the stone tablets on which were inscribed the Ten Commandments. Some accounts say Menelik stole the Ark. Others say Solomon gave the Ark as a gift, thus singling out Menelik's kingdom as unique and special in the eyes of God.

Many writings earlier than the *Kebra Negast* connect Ethiopia with the Ark of the Covenant and the

Queen of Sheba, naming Axum as her capital. Yekuno Amlak, who established the Solomonid dynasty, was the first to claim descent from Menelik. In his view he was restoring authority to its rightful lineage, as set forth by the will of God. Ethiopia's later emperors would assume power based on the same glorious ancestry.

Religious Battles and Power Struggles

Ethiopia's Christians soon faced yet another challenge. Portugal and Spain began sending Roman Catholic priests to Ethiopia. They pressed Ethiopians to convert from their Orthodox beliefs to Roman Catholicism. This resulted in centuries of bitterness between followers of Ethiopian and Roman Christianity.

Fasilidas's castle in Gondar

Emperor Susenyos converted to Roman Catholicism in 1622. This led to civil wars between Catholic and Orthodox Ethiopians. Susenyos grew weary of the conflicts and gave up the throne to his Orthodox son Fasilidas. Determined to shut out troublesome foreigners, Fasilidas closed Ethiopia to Europeans in 1632. He made the hilltop city of Gondar his capital. There he built a palace and the beautiful Debre Birhan Selassie (Holy Trinity) Church.

The 1700s brought more power struggles. Several emperors were assassinated, and regional princes wielded great power. Still, Christianity was a binding force that helped unite the people.

Tower in the courtyard of Debre Birhan Selassie Church

Menelik II

Menelik II was one of Ethiopia's greatest emperors. He established a new capital at Addis Ababa and united various regions until Ethiopia reached its present-day size. Hoping to modernize his country, he built telephone and telegraph systems, a railway, and a modern education system.

Under Menelik II, Ethiopia proved itself to be a strong military power. The northern province of Eritrea had become an Italian colony, and Italy set out to take over the rest of Ethiopia. In 1896, Menelik's army dealt the Italians a crushing defeat in the Battle of Adwa. It was a proud victory, for this was the first time an African army had ever defeated a European colonial power.

Menelik died in 1913, and his daughter Zauditu took the throne as empress in 1916. Her cousin Tafari Makonnen became regent, taking care of many governmental duties. Upon the empress's death in 1930, Tafari rose to the throne as Emperor Haile Selassie I.

The Second Menelik

Menelik II (1844–1913) was born as Sahle Miriam, son of the negus (king) of Shewa. Emperor Tewodros II invaded Shewa in 1855 and imprisoned Sahle for almost ten years. Sahle escaped and returned to Shewa, where he became negus himself. When Tewodros died in 1868, Sahle expected to become emperor. However, Tekle Giyorgis took power instead, followed by Yohannes IV in 1872. By the time Yohannes died in 1889, Sahle was Ethiopia's strongest leader, and he became emperor at last. He took the name Menelik II to confirm his authority.

Carving Up the Continent

In 1884, European powers met in Berlin, Germany, to divide up Africa among themselves. Many European nations were competing for trade rights in Africa, and the Berlin Conference (above) aimed to prevent war among rivals.

The resulting agreement was the Berlin Act of 1885. It carved Africa into dozens of states, with little regard for ethnic and cultural regions and with no input from the Africans themselves. Great Britain, France, Germany, Portugal, Belgium, Italy, and Spain were the major "winners." Some areas became colonies, while others became protectorates or possessions.

Italy occupied Eritrea in 1890 but hoped to claim the entire Horn of Africa. After suffering defeat in the 1896 Battle of Adwa, Italy was forced to recognize Ethiopia's independence.

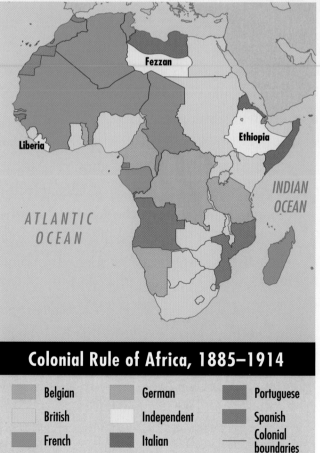

Fezzan

Ethiopia

Liberia

ATLANTIC OCEAN

INDIAN OCEAN

Colonial Rule of Africa, 1885–1914

- Belgian
- British
- French
- German
- Independent
- Italian
- Portuguese
- Spanish
- —— Colonial boundaries

Haile Selassie would be Ethiopia's last emperor. He continued to modernize the country, introducing a constitution, a two-house parliament, and a court system. He also outlawed Ethiopia's long-held practice of slavery and eliminated brutal punishments for crime.

Italian forces arrive in Ethiopia in 1935.

In 1963, Haile Salassie helped form the Organization of African Unity. This photo is from the 1993 OAU summit in Cairo, Egypt.

Italy's armies under Benito Mussolini invaded Ethiopia in 1935. They forced the emperor out, and he went into exile in England. On the way he made an impassioned plea to the League of Nations for help but was refused. The Italians united Ethiopia with Eritrea and Italian Somaliland to form Italian East Africa. Ethiopian patriots and British troops ousted the Italians in 1941, and Haile Selassie returned in triumph. Eritrea officially reunited with Ethiopia in 1952.

Haile Selassie was also a respected leader among African nations. In 1963, he helped form the Organization of African Unity (OAU). It made its headquarters in Addis Ababa. He also brought Ethiopia into the United Nations. In spite of his international leadership role, Haile Selassie was bitterly criticized at home. He was accused of spending lavishly on royal pleasures while ignoring his needy people and taxing them heavily. While he brought about many improvements in Ethiopia, they were not enough to relieve the country of its economic and social problems.

The Last Emperor

Ethiopia's last emperor was born as Tafari Makonnen. He took the name Haile Selassie, meaning "Power of the Trinity." He also took on the imperial titles King of Kings, Elect of God, Defender of the Faith, and Conquering Lion of the Tribe of Judah.

Haile Selassie (1892–1975), standing 5 feet 4 inches (1.6 m) tall, had a strong and dignified presence. His wife was Wayzaro Menen, a great-granddaughter of Menelik II. As a young man he was governor of Sidamo and Harer provinces, where he helped break the power of regional nobles. He gained much support among Ethiopia's Christians in 1916, when he deposed Menelik's grandson Lij Yasu, who had close ties to Ethiopian Muslims.

Ethiopia Under the Derg

An army officer, Mengistu Haile Mariam, led a military takeover in 1974. Haile Selassie was deposed, imprisoned, and probably murdered. The constitution and parliament were dissolved. A committee of soldiers called the Derg ruled the country, and Mengistu, as chairman of the Derg, became head of state.

This new regime tried to reshape Ethiopia into a socialist state, with banks and businesses under government control. Private farmland was grouped into collective farms worked by all the villagers in an area, and thousands of people were relocated. Mengistu unleashed a "red terror" against his opponents, torturing and killing people across the country.

Eritrea and Tigray were also fighting to pull away from Ethiopia and form their own governments, and Ethiopian

Lieutenant Colonel Mengistu Haile Mariam became head of state when he led a military takeover in 1974.

Refugees seeking relief at a camp during Ethiopia's worst famine

Somalis were rebelling, too. The Soviet Union and Cuba sent military aid. In the midst of this political upheaval, Ethiopia suffered the worst famine in its history. In 1984 and 1985, more than 1 million Ethiopians starved to death. Many countries hesitated to send aid because of Ethiopia's military regime and civil wars. Emergency food supplies often went to the military instead of the famine victims. The Derg had brought Ethiopia to the brink of disaster.

The Democratic Republic

In 1991, a group called the Ethiopian People's Revolutionary Democratic Front (EPRDF) marched into Addis Ababa and took control of the government. Leading them was Meles Zenawi, who became the temporary president. Just a few months later, the Eritrean People's Liberation Front (EPLF) took control of Eritrea. Eritreans voted for independence in 1993, and the Ethiopian government approved. Ethiopia introduced a new constitution in 1994 and declared itself a democratic republic.

Ethiopian rebels break through the entrance of the Presidential Palace as they take Addis Ababa in 1991.

Troubles with Eritrea were far from over. The two powers had never quite agreed on a border, and this dispute exploded into a full-scale war in 1998. Two years of fighting left more than eighty thousand people dead. Ethiopia and Eritrea signed a peace agreement in December 2000, with the border still in question. An international commission marked the boundary, but Ethiopia disputed its ruling, and border clashes began again in 2002.

Ethiopia remains one of the world's poorest countries, with millions of people barely making a living. Poverty, health care, regional conflicts, and economic development will remain Ethiopia's greatest challenges in the years to come.

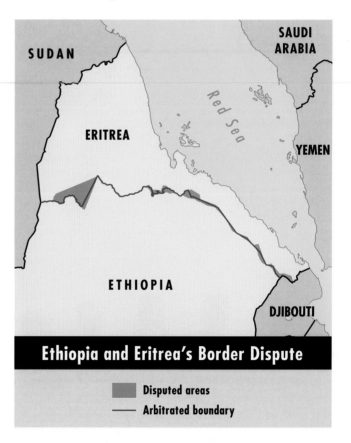

Ethiopia and Eritrea's Border Dispute

- Disputed areas
- Arbitrated boundary

Governing
the Republic

E THIOPIA'S OFFICIAL NAME IS THE FEDERAL DEMOCRATIC Republic of Ethiopia (FDRE). The nation adopted its present constitution in 1995. It declares that Ethiopia has a parliamentary form of government. This is similar to the British system, with power centered in a two-house parliament. The constitution also guarantees equal rights to people of both genders and all religions and ethnic groups. All citizens are entitled to vote at age eighteen.

Opposite: **In 1995, Ethiopia adopted its current constitution. It grants equal rights to all citizens.**

The National Flag

Ethiopia's flag features three horizontal bars—green, yellow, and red. In the center of the flag is a light blue disk. Upon it is a five-pointed yellow star, with rays extending out between the points.

The color green stands for Ethiopia's fertile land. Yellow represents Ethiopia's religious freedom. Red stands for the many lives given up to protect the country. Because Ethiopia was Africa's first independent nation, many other African states adopted these colors when they gained independence. Thus, these three colors—green, yellow, and red—became known as the pan-African colors.

The blue disk stands for Ethiopia's peace and prosperity. The star's points, at an equal distance from one another, attest to the equality of all Ethiopia's ethnic groups, faiths, and genders. The shining rays are the promise of a bright future. Ethiopia adopted this flag on February 6, 1996.

A plain, three-color flag—with red at the top and without the center emblem—first appeared in 1897. During Haile Selassie's reign the Lion of Judah emblem was added to the center. The lion had a golden crown on its head and carried a cross-shaped scepter from which a banner waved. Even today, this lion represents the emperors' descent from King Solomon and the Queen of Sheba. From 1987 to 1991, during Mengistu's presidency, the center emblem consisted of a star shining over a monument of the Axumite kingdom and a cogwheel, or machine gear.

The parliament building houses the Federal Parliamentary Assembly.

The Legislature

The Federal Parliamentary Assembly is Ethiopia's parliament. It is the country's legislature, or lawmaking body. Like the British Parliament and the U.S. Congress, it is made up of two houses. The upper house is the House of the Federation. It has the power to interpret the constitution. Its 108 members are elected by the state councils, or legislatures of the various states. The lower house is the House of People's Representatives, which makes Ethiopia's laws. This house may have up to 550 members. They are elected by the nation's

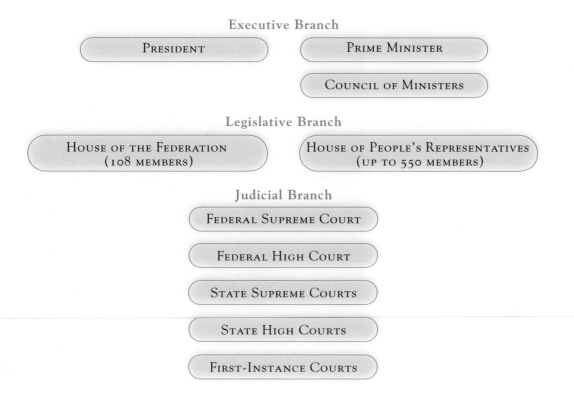

NATIONAL GOVERNMENT OF ETHIOPIA

Executive Branch

PRESIDENT

PRIME MINISTER

COUNCIL OF MINISTERS

Legislative Branch

HOUSE OF THE FEDERATION
(108 MEMBERS)

HOUSE OF PEOPLE'S REPRESENTATIVES
(UP TO 550 MEMBERS)

Judicial Branch

FEDERAL SUPREME COURT

FEDERAL HIGH COURT

STATE SUPREME COURTS

STATE HIGH COURTS

FIRST-INSTANCE COURTS

voters according to population. Members of both houses serve five-year terms.

The constitution makes sure that all of Ethiopia's nationalities and ethnic groups have representatives in the legislature. The House of the Federation must include at least one member from each of twenty-two nationalities or ethnic groups. An additional representative is granted for each one million members of that group. The House of People's Representatives must include at least twenty members of minority nationalities and groups.

Meles Zenawi

Meles Zenawi (1956–) was born in Adwa in the Tigray region. In 1974, he joined the Tigray People's Liberation Front (TPLF) to fight the Derg military regime. He eventually became chairman of the TPLF. In 1989, he helped bring about an alliance of regional groups opposing the Derg. This alliance became the Ethiopian People's Revolutionary Democratic Front (EPRDF), and Meles served as its chairman.

After Mengistu was deposed in 1991, Meles became president of Ethiopia's transitional government. In 1995, he was elected the first prime minister of the Federal Democratic Republic of Ethiopia.

The Executive

The prime minister is Ethiopia's chief executive and head of government. The prime minister is chosen by the House of People's Representatives and comes from whichever political party holds the majority of seats there. The prime minister serves a five-year term and usually stays in office as long as his or her party is in power. The prime minister appoints a council of ministers to oversee various areas such as foreign affairs, health, education, agriculture, and defense.

Ethiopia's president is the head of state. The president is elected by a two-thirds majority vote in the full legislature and holds office for six years, with a two-term limit. The president's duties are mainly ceremonial. For example, the president calls the legislature to order, appoints ambassadors, and grants pardons. With the approval of the prime minister, the president can also grant high military titles to deserving officers.

The Judicial System

The Federal Supreme Court is Ethiopia's highest court. The second-highest court is the Federal High Court. Both courts handle cases involving federal laws, national security, and issues that cross regional boundaries. Judges in both courts are appointed by the House of People's Representatives and serve until the age of sixty.

The Federal Supreme Court is divided into three sections—civil, criminal, and military. It oversees all the courts

National Anthem of Ethiopia

"Whedefit Gesgeshi Woude Henate Ethiopia"
("March Forward, Dear Mother Ethiopia")
Adopted in 1992
Words by Dereje Melaku Mengesha (1957–), music by Solomon Lulu Mitiku (1950–).

Respect for citizenship is strong in our Ethiopia;
National pride is seen, shining from one side to another.
For peace, for justice, for the freedom of peoples,
In equality and in love we stand united.
Firm of foundation, we do not dismiss humanness;
We are peoples who live through work.
Wonderful is the stage of tradition, mistress of proud heritage,
Mother of natural virtue, mother of a valorous people.
We shall protect you—we have a duty;
Our Ethiopia, live! And let us be proud of you!

in the country. It also reviews cases in which there might have been errors made in court proceedings. The Federal High Court hears appeals from lower courts. As a last resort, a High Court ruling can be appealed to the Supreme Court.

Each of Ethiopia's regional states can establish a State Supreme Court, a High Court, and a First-Instance Court. Traditional courts settle local disputes in many rural areas. These courts lessen the caseloads of the higher courts, which are often backlogged with cases. Shari'a courts, or Islamic courts, may handle cases involving religious or family matters among Muslims.

Regional Government

Ethiopia is divided into nine states. As much as possible, their boundaries have been drawn according to the ethnic and language groups of the people in each region. This is not a perfect division, though. Some ethnic groups spread across a wide area, and state boundaries cut through their territories.

The nine regional states are Tigray, Afar, Amhara, Oromia, Somalia, Benishangul-Gumuz, Gambela, Harari, and the State of Southern Nations, Nationalities, and Peoples (SNNP). Each regional state has a president and a state council. The regional states are further divided into administrative zones and *woredas*, or subzones.

The cities of Addis Ababa and Dire Dawa have separate governments of their own. They are called chartered cities. Addis Ababa has a chairman and a city council. Dire Dawa is governed by a chairman and an administrative council.

A Voice for Everyone

Ethiopia has dozens of political parties. Many of them promote the interests of one nationality or ethnic group. For example, there are political parties representing the Amhara, Tigray, Oromo, Somali, Sidama, Gurage, Afar, Konso, and many other groups.

Two or more parties with similar goals often join together to form an alliance. With more members, the newly created party then becomes a more powerful force in the legislature. This is what happened after the EPRDF was formed in 1989. (See the sidebar below for parties' full names.) This alliance became Ethiopia's majority party. Its chairman, Meles Zenawi, headed the transitional government in 1991. He was elected the first prime minister of democratic Ethiopia in 1995.

Some of Ethiopia's political parties want independence for their people. Some want to unite their ethnic groups with those in neighboring countries. Some simply want fair treatment and equal rights. Regardless of their goals, they all have a voice in the legislature.

Political Parties: An Alphabet Soup

The abbreviations for Ethiopia's political parties have been called an alphabet soup. Here are just a few of the current parties and their abbreviations.

ANDM	Amhara National Democratic Movement (represents the Amhara people)
CEOPO	Coalition of Ethiopian Opposition Political Organizations
EDUP	Ethiopian Democratic Unity Party
EPRDF	Ethiopian People's Revolutionary Democratic Front (an alliance of the ANDM, OPDO, and TPLF)
OPDO	Oromo People's Democratic Organization (represents the Oromo people)
SPDP	Somali People's Democratic Party (an alliance of a dozen groups)
TPLF	Tigray People's Liberation Front (dominant group in the EPRDF)

Addis Ababa: Did You Know This?

Addis Ababa is a bustling city with tall office buildings and cozy coffee shops, as well as traditional homes with grazing areas for sheep and goats nearby. Eucalyptus trees line the wide city streets. Churchill Road is the main downtown avenue. At its north end stands the City Council building. The surrounding area is called the Piazza, a district of fine restaurants and shops. On the other extreme is the colorful Mercato, to the west. This open-air market is one of the largest in Africa (right).

Addis Ababa is Ethiopia's cultural center. It is home to Addis Ababa University, the university's Ethnological Museum, and the National Museum, or Archaeological Museum. The city also serves as the headquarters for the United Nations Economic Commission for Africa (ECA) and the African Union (AU), which used to be

called the Organization of African Unity (OAU). Both are housed in the magnificent Africa Hall. Nearby is the National Palace, built during Haile Selassie's reign. The national government offices are in Menelik Palace, built in 1887.

Location: In the center of the country, on a plateau at the base of the Entoto Mountains

Population (2004 est.): 2,763,500

Founded: 1887

Founder: Emperor Menelik II

Meaning of Name: "New Flower"

Altitude: About 8,000 feet (2,438 m) above sea level

Highest Average Temperature: 65.1°F (18.4°C) in May

Lowest Average Temperature: 60.3°F (15.7°C) in November

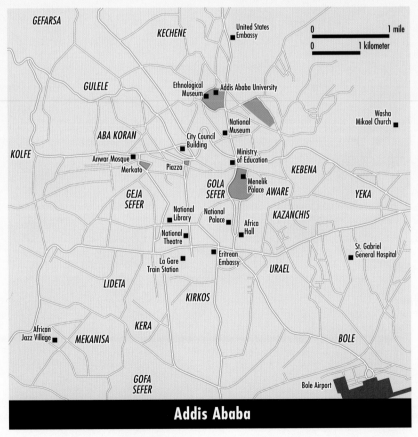

Addis Ababa

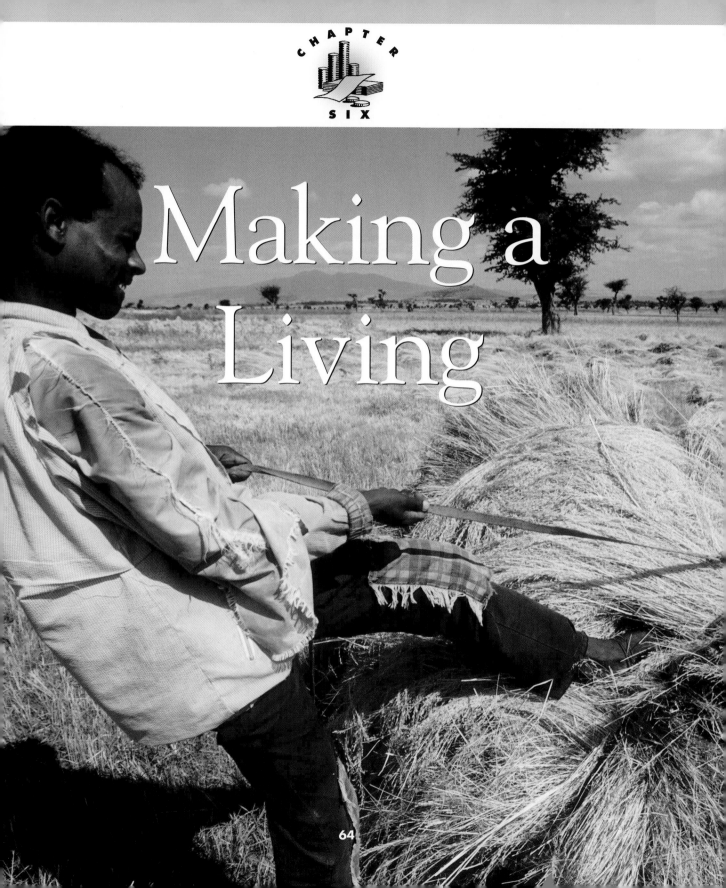

Making a Living

A YOUNG MAN IN ADDIS ABABA IS PROUD OF HIS BUSI-
ness. "I sell goats," he says. This is not unusual. In
marketplaces around the country, people are selling goats. But
he found a different way to market his goods. He sells goats on
his Internet site. His customers are Ethiopians living outside
the country. If they want to send a goat to their families back
home, they can order it on the Web.

This young man is one of many Ethiopians who have created profitable businesses. They are the lucky ones. On the
other extreme are the people who can barely feed their families. Overall, Ethiopia is a desperately poor country. The
United Nations ranks it as one of the poorest, least-developed
countries in the world.
Almost two-thirds of the
population lives on less
than U.S.$1 a day.

Agriculture is Ethiopia's
major industry, but it is
subject to the whims of
the weather. Rains may
fall too late, too heavily, or
too sparsely. Drought is a
constant danger, especially
in the arid east and the
far north.

Opposite: **Earning a living in
Ethiopia ranges from being
a service worker to working
in factories or on farms. This
man is harvesting and
bundling wheat.**

**Farming is Ethiopia's biggest
industry. However, the country relies on food aid from
international organizations.**

An Ancient Grain

Teff is Ethiopia's most important food crop. Ethiopians were raising teff as early as 3300 B.C. Teff's tiny, round grains are high in protein, minerals, fiber, and other essential nutrients. Its name may have come from the Amharic word meaning "lost," because the grain is so small.

Teff is used to make a traditional flatbread called *injera*. It is also popular as a baby food because of its nutritional value. The stalks are used for animal feed and for making thatched roofs and mud bricks. Teff is becoming a popular health food in the United States.

Today's government is moving ahead with plans for preventing future disasters. Many foreign organizations are working with farmers, too. New irrigation systems, hardier crops, and more efficient equipment are all helping farmers to make a secure living. Meanwhile, Ethiopia still depends heavily on food aid from international agencies.

Crops and Animals

Most farming in Ethiopia takes place on small family farms. More than four out of five residents make their living by farming. Grains are Ethiopia's major crops, covering about four-fifths of the cultivated land. A grain called teff is the leading food crop. It is grown mainly in the cool highlands. Maize (corn), wheat, sorghum, barley, and millet are some of the country's other grain crops.

Farmers also raise coffee, cotton, sugarcane, oilseeds, vegetables, and fruits. Both family farms and large plantations grow trees such as banana, papaya, and *ensete*. The ensete tree is locally called "false banana," because it looks very much like a banana tree. Shavings cut from its roots and trunk are used to make a type of bread.

Ethiopia has more livestock, or farm animals, than any other African country. This includes cattle, sheep, goats, donkeys, horses, and camels. These animals provide their owners with meat, milk, and hides. They also yield many valuable export products, such as leather goods and processed meats. And don't forget the bees. Honey is an important product both for home use and for export.

A herder guides his cattle through a village. Farm animals are a good source of meat and milk for their owners.

Weights and Measures

The metric system is Ethiopia's official system of weights and measures. But people in rural areas often use traditional measures. For example, the traditional unit for measuring land is the *gasha* (99 acres/40 hectares). A gasha was once considered the area that one family needed to survive. The *enqib*, for measuring grain, is about one bushel. The *tassa*, for liquids, is about 1 liter (1.06 quarts).

Many traditional measures depend on the size of the person taking the measure. A *kend*, for instance, is the distance from the tip of the elbow to the tip of the middle finger.

The Coffee Business

Most farmers in Ethiopia raise food to eat themselves, rather than to sell. Coffee is the major exception. Most of Ethiopia's coffee is sold to other countries. As Ethiopia's major export, it brings in more than half the nation's export income.

Money Facts

Ethiopia's Axumite kingdom minted bronze and silver coins, some of them inlaid with gold. Today, the birr is Ethiopia's basic unit of currency. One birr is divided into 100 cents. Banknotes are issued in values of 1, 5, 10, 50, and 100 birr. Coins come in values of 1, 5, 10, 25, and 50 cents. In November 2004, US$1.00 was equal to 8.434 birr, and 1 birr was equal to US$0.119.

Ethiopia's banknotes highlight the country's industries and natural beauty. For example, the 1-birr note shows a young man with longhorn cattle in the background. On the reverse side is a scene of the Blue Nile Falls. A coffee worker and the native animals kudu and caracal appear on the 5-birr note. The 10-birr note features a basket weaver and a farmer. The 100-birr note contrasts Ethiopia's traditional and modern cultures. It shows a farmer guiding an ox-drawn plow and a scientist peering through a microscope.

Ethiopia's arabica coffee beans come in thousands of varieties, with flavors ranging from spicy to chocolatey to flowery. After the beans are harvested, they go to one of more than four hundred coffee-processing plants. There they are sorted and washed. Samples from each day's production are brewed into a beverage, and professional tasters drink them to check for quality.

Then workers load sacks of coffee beans onto trucks and take them to auction centers in Addis Ababa or Dire Dawa, where buyers from all over the world travel to purchase coffee by the truckload.

Some of the world's best coffee is grown in Ethiopia. It is the country's major export.

Service Industries

Services are Ethiopia's second-biggest industry after agriculture. Service workers include people who work in stores and shops, banks, government offices, and the army. Teachers,

Kaldi and the Dancing Goats

According to legend, a goatherd named Kaldi was grazing his goats on a mountainside. At the end of the day, the goats were nowhere to be found.

After searching for hours, Kaldi discovered them dancing and prancing wildly around an evergreen bush, whose red berries they had been eating. Kaldi tasted the berries himself and soon he, too, was frolicking with delight.

Kaldi took some berries to show to the monks in a nearby monastery. One monk declared the berries to be the work of the devil and flung them into the fire. Such a delicious aroma arose that the monks rescued the berries, ground them, and made them into the hot, black drink we know as coffee. This beverage must be a gift from God, the monks decided, for it kept the faithful awake for their prayers.

After agriculture, the service industry ranks as Ethiopia's second-largest industry. Service workers include teachers such as this one.

SAUDI ARABIA

Red Sea

ERITREA

SUDAN

YEMEN

K
Salt
Gonder   Gyp
S   Salt   Gulf of Aden

DJIBOUTI

Ls   Dese
Ls   Marb
Gyp Dire
S   Dawa

Marb   Wheat   Addis Ababa
Au   Pt Barley   SOMALIA
Corn   Nazret
Asb   Ls

Sheep and
Goats

Au
Ls

SOMALIA

UGANDA   KENYA

Resources

▨ Forests	Nomadic livestock herding	Pasture livestock
Asb **Asbestos**	K **Potash**	Pt **Platinum**
Au **Gold**	Ls **Limestone**	S **Sulfur**
Gyp **Gypsum**	Marb **Marble**	Salt **Salt**

health care workers, and truck and taxi drivers are service workers, too. Banking and government are the largest service industries, and they are centered in the capital city.

Factories and Mines

Manufacturing is a growing industry in Ethiopia. Most factory goods are made from farm products. For example, cotton is made into cotton fabric, the leading factory product. Flour from wheat and other grains is processed to make pasta. Hides from farm animals are cut and shaped into shoes and sandals. Other livestock products are milk, butter, cheese, and canned and frozen meats. Ethiopia's factories also produce beer and wine, chemicals, cement, and metal goods.

In ancient times, Ethiopians mined gold and traded it to the Egyptians. Today, Ethiopia's Legadembi Gold Mine is a leading source of gold for export. Many other valuable minerals lie underground. Platinum, copper, and lead are just a few examples. Ethiopia's marble and limestone are important construction materials. Kaolin, gypsum, and silica are used in various industries. Mines on the Danakil Plain yield sulfur, salts, gypsum, and potash.

Workers cut blocks of salt on the Danakil Plain.

What Ethiopia Grows, Makes, and Mines

Agriculture (2002)

Teff and other grains	9,096,300 metric tons
Potatoes and other roots and tubers	4,724,000 metric tons
Coffee	220,000 metric tons

Manufacturing (2000–2001)

Cotton fabrics	45,000,000 square meters
Leather footwear	6,358,000 pairs
Beer	1,605,000 hectoliters

Mining

Gold (2000/2001)	5,200 kilograms
Limestone (2000/2001)	1,300,000 metric tons
Marble (1998/1999)	152,000 cubic meters

Ethiopia imports the petroleum (oil) it needs for fuel. Large deposits of oil have been discovered in western Ethiopia. The country has natural gas reserves, too. However, like many of Ethiopia's other mineral resources, they have not been developed yet. In time these minerals could provide good income for the country.

Getting Around

"Every tourist helps forty Ethiopians," says Yusuf Abdullahi Sukkar, Ethiopia's tourism commissioner. He sees tourism as a realistic way to bring more money into the country. Yusuf explains that each tourist brings income to at least forty people who conduct tours, sell supplies, or work in hotels and restaurants.

Reports of civil wars and famine kept tourists away from Ethiopia for years. Now tourism is growing, although it is not always easy for tourists to get around. Rough roads and mountainous land can make it hard to travel and transport goods.

Many Ethiopians earn money by giving tours or working in hotels and restaurants.

A small percentage of Ethiopia's roadways are paved. Mountain passes make for a difficult trek for merchants.

Only about 15 percent of Ethiopia's roads are paved. They include a major highway running from Addis Ababa south into Kenya. Other roads may be gravel or well-trod dirt. People, animals, and vehicles have also worn miles of tracks and trails through the countryside.

The government owns Ethiopian Airlines, the national airline. It flies to many locations within Ethiopia as well as to dozens of foreign cities. Addis Ababa's Bole International Airport has a brand-new terminal, with a glass roof and Tigrayan marble floors. Dire Dawa also has an international airport, and many towns have airfields or landing strips.

When Eritrea became independent, Ethiopia lost its seaports. Now Ethiopia is a landlocked country. It used to ship goods into and out of Assab and Massawa, in Eritrea. Now Ethiopia trades through the port of Djibouti, a small republic at the mouth of the Red Sea. A railroad line runs between Djibouti and Addis Ababa.

Keeping in Touch

In 1897, Emperor Menelik II picked up a telephone in Addis Ababa and called Haile Selassie's father, Ras Makonnen, in Harer. The emperor was testing his country's newly installed telephone system. Ethiopia's telephone service has grown tremendously since then, but it has a long way to go. In 2002, there were only about 353,800 telephones in Ethiopia. That's about one phone for every two hundred people. More than fifty thousand cell phones were in use, though.

Most of the country's fifty thousand Internet subscribers live in Addis Ababa, and most users are businesses and government offices. Meanwhile, the government is working to bring Internet service to rural areas. Internet cafés stand among the roadside shops in major cities and towns.

For daily news, the most widely read newspaper is *Addis Zemen*, in the Amharic language. English-language daily papers are the *Ethiopian Herald* and *The Daily Monitor*. The *Addis Tribune* is one of many weekly papers. However, most people find out what's happening through radio and television. Ethiopian Television is the only television station. The major radio station, Radio Ethiopia, broadcasts in several languages.

One Land, Many Peoples

H OW MANY PEOPLE LIVE IN ETHIOPIA?
In 2004, the estimated population was 72
million. It is hard to make an accurate
count, though. Many Ethiopians who fled
the country because of wars or famines are
coming back. At the same time, people who
fled from neighboring countries to Ethiopia
for the same reasons are going back home.
No one can keep track of all these shifts or
the many unreported births and deaths.

Most Ethiopians live in scattered villages across the rural countryside. Only
about one out of every six people lives in a
city or town. Addis Ababa is the capital and
largest city. Next in size is Dire Dawa,
toward the east. It has long been a trade center—first on the
caravan routes and later on the rail line to Djibouti. Some of
the other large cities are Nazret, Gondar, Mekele, Bahir Dar,
and Dese.

Most Ethiopians live in the
countryside rather than in
urban areas.

A Multiethnic Society

Ethiopia is truly a multiethnic society. It is home to more
than eighty different ethnic groups, or tribes. For many of
them, regional boundaries do not necessarily show where they
live. Ethiopia's state and national borders often cross right

Opposite: **Ethiopia is multiethnic, with more than
eighty ethnic groups living
within its borders.**

One Land, Many Peoples **77**

The map legend:

Persons per square mile	Persons per square kilometer
518–1033	200–399
260–517	100–199
130–259	50–99
65–129	25–49
25–64	10–24
3–24	1–9
fewer than 3	fewer than 1

The largest ethnic group in Ethiopia is the Oromo.

through a group's traditional homeland. This is why some ethnic groups want to pull away and join other countries or form nations of their own. Still, certain groups are clustered in specific regions.

The Oromo are the largest group, accounting for about one-third of the population. They live mainly in central, southern, eastern, and western Ethiopia. Many Oromo live by farming and herding.

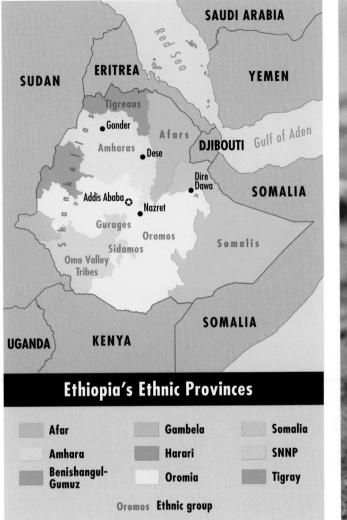

Ethiopia's Ethnic Provinces

Afar	Gambela	Somalia
Amhara	Harari	SNNP
Benishangul-Gumuz	Oromia	Tigray

Oromos **Ethnic group**

Young Amhara shepherd

Amharic and Tigrean people, who are related to each other, make up a little more than one-third of the population. They live mainly on the northern plateau. Tigreans live the farthest north, spilling over into Eritrea. The Gurage, who are largely merchants, are dispersed throughout the country. The Sidama occupy south-central Ethiopia, living mostly as farmers.

Ethnic Groups (1994 census)	
Oromo	32%
Amhara	30%
Tigrean	6.2%
Somali	6%
Gurage	4.3%
Sidama	3.5%
Others	18%

Afar women

The eastern "horn" of Ethiopia, surrounded by Somalia, is the homeland of ethnic Somalis. Northeastern Ethiopia is home to the Afars, who also live in neighboring Djibouti and Eritrea. They live as nomadic herders.

People from dozens of ethnic groups live in the west and southwest. Many groups in the far west are related to peoples living across the border in Sudan. More than forty ethnic groups live in the regional state called Southern Nations, Nationalities, and Peoples.

The Omo Valley Tribes

The lower Omo River valley, in the far southwest, is home to dozens of distinct tribes. Many live in or near Mago and Omo national parks, which border the river.

One tribe, the Karo (right), has only about 1,500 members left. Others include the Arbore, Ari, Banna, Bodi, Bumi, Dizi, Hamar, Kaygu, Mursi, Surma, and Tsamai. They may live as farmers, cattle herders, or both. Each group has its characteristic culture, clothing, body decorations, and beliefs.

It is sometimes difficult to classify Ethiopians according to their ethnic groups. There are many factors that make up a person's ethnic identity—race, language, religion, customs, region, and historical experience. Different ethnic groups may share a language or religion. At the same time one ethnic group may include people with different religions or ways of life. Thus Ethiopians are often grouped according to the language they speak.

Land of Many Tongues

If you traveled all over Ethiopia, you would hear about eighty-two languages, with two hundred dialects, or variations. Each

Population of Major Cities	
(2004 estimates; metropolitan area only)	
Addis Ababa	2,763,500
Dire Dawa	254,500
Nazret	176,800
Gondar	147,900
Mekele	133,500
Bahir Dar	131,800
Dese	126,300
Jimma	117,600
Harer	99,600

Ethiopia is a land of many languages. It is not uncommon for Ethiopians to speak more than one language.

ethnic group has its own language, and speakers in different areas have their own unique dialects. Many Ethiopians speak more languages than the one they learned at home. They can communicate in other Ethiopian languages as well as in foreign languages.

Ethiopia's official language is Amharic. It is used in most government and business situations. It has served as the official

Naming System

Both men and women in Ethiopia use their father's name as their surname, or family name. A woman does not change her name when she marries. She keeps her surname and simply changes her title from Woizerit (Miss) to Woizero (Mrs.). A man's title is Ato (Mr.).

Ethiopians are addressed by their first name, or given name. A man named Tsegaye Desta would be called Ato Tsegaye. An unmarried woman named Almaz Teferra would be called Woizerit Almaz. If she married, she would become Woizero Almaz.

language for centuries. The culture of the Amharic-speaking ruling class became the dominant culture, and their language became widespread.

English is the most widely spoken foreign language. Classes in secondary schools and universities are conducted in English. English is often used in government and business, too. Some Ethiopians also speak French or Arabic.

As Ethiopia's many ethnic groups focus on their cultural identities, they are using their own languages more and more. Besides Amharic, other widely spoken languages are Oromifa (or Orominga), spoken by the Oromo; Tigrinya, the language of the Tigreans and an official language in Eritrea; Guaraginga, spoken by the Gurage; and Somali, the language of Somali people.

Tigrinya is closely related to Amharic. In fact, both languages use the same script, or form of writing. Both Amharic and Tigrinya are also related to an ancient language called Ge'ez. It was the language of the Axumite kingdom. Today, Ge'ez is the language used in Ethiopian Orthodox Church services.

Pronouncing Amharic

Some sounds in Amharic don't exist in English. Here are the seven vowel sounds with rough pronunciations. (It is best to hear a native Amharic speaker!) Notice that there are three different sounds that we spell as *e*.

Vowel	Pronunciation
e	as in *her*, without the *r*
u	as in *flute*
i	as in *bit*
a	as in *father*
e	as in *bed*
e	as in *the*, but very short
o	as in *hot*

Most Amharic consonants are pronounced as the consonants are in English. However, there are more consonant sounds in Amharic than the Roman alphabet can spell. Here are some of the differing consonant sounds.

Consonant	Pronunciation
ch	as in *chew*
ch	as in *witch*, with a longer, accented *tch*
k	as in *kit*
k	as in *yuck*, with a throaty, accented *ck*
ny	as in *canyon*
p	as in *pit*
p	as in *pot*, with a short, popping *p*
s	as in *sit*
s	as in *miss*, with a longer, hissing *s*
t	as in *time*, with the tongue touching the teeth
t	as in *hot*, with an explosive, "spitting" *t*
t	as in *butter*, with a longer, accented *tt*
zh	as in *pleasure*

Common Amharic Words and Phrases

Selam (seh-LAHM)	Hello (peace be with you)
Tenastilign/tenastelen (teh-NAH-steh-lehn)	Hello (may you have good health)
Denaneh?/denanesh? (deh-NAH-neh/deh-NAH-nesh)	How are you? (to a man/woman)
Dehna nenyi (DEH-nah NEHN-yee)	I'm fine
Dehna hun/hunyi (DEH-nah HOON/HOON-yee)	Good-bye (to a man/woman)
Ow (OW)	Yes
Aye or *aydelem* (EYE or EYE-deh-lehm)	No
Amesegenalew (ah-meh-seh-geh-NAH-lew)	Thank you

The Written Language

Amharic is a Semitic language, just as Arabic and Hebrew are. Unlike most Semitic languages, however, Amharic is written from left to right.

The Ethiopic alphabet was adapted from the Ge'ez script. This set of characters is not really an alphabet but a syllabary.

This billboard in Addis Ababa is written in Amharic as well as English.

That is, each character stands for a syllable made up of a consonant and a vowel. The Ethiopic syllabary has thirty-three basic characters. Most of these characters stand for consonant sounds. Each character has seven different forms. They are created by adding a stroke, or squiggle, to the basic character or changing its shape slightly. These variations show which of seven vowel sounds should be pronounced in that syllable. As a result the full array of Ethiopic characters comes to a total of 231!

Naturally, many non-Ethiopians have an easier time reading the Roman (Western) alphabet than Ethiopic script. Thus, Amharic is often transliterated, or Romanized, to spell out Amharic sounds. Since there are many different transliteration systems, one Amharic word may have different spellings when written in the Roman alphabet. Unfortunately, when Amharic is transliterated, some information about pronunciation is lost. Our alphabet cannot really capture all the unique Amharic sounds.

Health Conditions

Based on past statistics, a newborn child in Ethiopia can expect to live for forty-six years. Poor nutrition and a lack of proper medical care have a lot to do with this short life span. Diseases such as malaria, yellow fever, and influenza take many lives every year. The larger cities have hospitals, and clinics operate in many rural areas. However, people often do not have a way to travel to them.

Another health problem is AIDS (acquired immune deficiency syndrome). Many thousands of Ethiopians are afflicted with the disease. The government is waging an aggressive campaign to promote AIDS awareness and prevention. Part of this effort goes toward posting educational posters and billboards in rural areas.

The World Health Organization (WHO), the United Nations, and many private organizations are also working to improve Ethiopia's health conditions. They provide food and medicine, as well as education in health, nutrition, and farming practices.

CHAPTER EIGHT

The Life of the Spirit

O N ANY DAY IN ETHIOPIA, YOU ARE LIKELY TO SEE CROWDS of devout, white-robed people. They may be clustered around a house of worship, gathered under a tree for prayer, filing in procession, or trekking to a pilgrimage site. Religion has been a major force in Ethiopia's history. And today, as always, religious beliefs are an important part of Ethiopians' daily lives.

Ethiopia's two major religions are Ethiopian Orthodox Christianity and Islam. There is much disagreement about how many people hold these two faiths. Some sources say Christians are in the majority, while others say there are more Muslims. It is hard to make an accurate count, as not all believers are officially registered. In any case, these two religions account for about 90 percent of Ethiopia's population.

A small portion of the population follows traditional native beliefs. They may honor one god or a variety of spirits. Small communities of Protestants and Roman Catholics are also found in Ethiopia, as well as Hindus and Sikhs. Most Ethiopian Jews had left the country by 1999 (see page 103).

Opposite: **Religion plays a major role in Ethiopia. Here the clergy walk beneath decorated umbrellas during the Timkat celebration.**

Religions of Ethiopia

Ethiopian Orthodox	40–45%
Islam	40–45%
Indigenous Religions	7–12%
Other	3–8%

Ethiopian Orthodox Christianity

The Ethiopian Orthodox Church, called Tewahido in Ethiopia, is one of the oldest forms of Christianity in the world. It flourished long before Christianity took hold in

Western Europe. The faith came to Ethiopia from Egypt, where Christians belonged to the Coptic Church.

Around A.D. 330, Frumentius, called the Apostle of Ethiopia, converted the Axumite king Ezana. The king declared Christianity the empire's official religion. Frumentius went on to build churches and spread the faith throughout the kingdom.

Ethiopia was isolated from the rest of the Christian world for centuries. Even ties with Egypt's church grew thin. Gradually, Christianity in Ethiopia developed into the form known today as the Ethiopian Orthodox Church. It developed a unique set of beliefs, including emphasis on the Old Testament and on Jewish traditions, as well as influences from indigenous religions.

The head of the Ethiopian Orthodox Church is the patriarch, who lives in Addis Ababa. He is known as the Abune, which means "father." Beneath him are archbishops and bishops for different sections of the country. Priests and deacons

Abune Paulos

Patriarch Paulos, or Abune Paulos (1935–), became the patriarch of the Ethiopian Orthodox Church in 1992. He was imprisoned from 1975 to 1983 under Ethiopia's Derg regime, allegedly for political reasons. After his release Paulos lived as a refugee in the United States. Since he became patriarch, he has worked hard for peace between Ethiopia and Eritrea. He has also helped the Orthodox Church to play a greater role as a relief organization for Ethiopia's drought and war victims.

A monk in his cell in Lalibela

conduct religious services, which are traditionally in the ancient Ge'ez language. Today, however, some churches are using modern Amharic.

Monasteries

Monasteries are an important tradition in the Ethiopian Orthodox Church. They are both spiritual and intellectual centers. While priests marry, monks do not. They lead lives devoted to prayer and religious study. Their daily routine may begin with prayer from midnight until dawn and may include eating only one meal a day. In Lalibela and other sites, the monks live in "cells" that are only holes in a rock.

Pilgrims wait their turn to climb a rope that will take them up to Debre Damo monastery.

Many monasteries and churches were built high on mountaintops or cliffs. This kept them safe in times of persecution. Debre Damo monastery, for example, is perched on the edge of a cliff. It can be reached only by climbing up the cliff with the help of ropes.

The largest cluster of monasteries stands on the islands and shores of Lake Tana. Ura Kidane Mehret is on the lake's Zege Peninsula. Inside its church, massive walls surround the center chamber, reaching from the floor to far overhead. They are covered with religious paintings executed in rich, vivid colors. Like many of Ethiopia's religious treasures, they are in danger of deterioration from the weather.

Religious paintings decorate the walls of Ura Kidane Mehret monastery.

The Tale of the Ark

According to Judeo-Christian tradition, Moses built the Ark of the Covenant to house the stone tablets of the Ten Commandments, which were given to him by God. King Solomon enshrined the Ark in his temple in Jerusalem.

Scholars are not absolutely sure what became of the Ark after that. Some believe it was moved to a Jewish temple on Elephantine Island, off the coast of Egypt, in the seventh century B.C. This temple was destroyed around 410 B.C. After that, Jews took the Ark up the Nile River and into the Ethiopian highlands for safety.

This theory connects somewhat with Ethiopian Orthodox tradition. According to church beliefs, Menelik took the Ark from Jerusalem to Ethiopia. Visitors to the Chapel of the Ark (below) in Axum are not allowed into the inner chamber where the Ark rests. A lone monk stands guard for life over its precious contents.

Priests lead a procession around the Ark of the Covenant chapel during a religious service.

Devotions

The Ark of the Covenant holds a special place in the spiritual life of the faithful. To many, it is a symbol that they are the chosen people of God. The original Ark itself is believed to rest in a chapel of Axum's Saint Mary of Zion Church.

The focal point of every Ethiopian Orthodox church is the *tabot*—a chest containing a stone tablet—which represents the Ark of the Covenant. It rests in the Holy of Holies, an inner chamber where only priests and monks may enter.

The Mass, or Eucharist service (*Qidasse*), is the most important church rite. Most of the Mass is sung or chanted, with drums, rattles, and sticks marking the rhythm. Services are most elaborate on major feast days. They last all through the night and into the next day, with the priest dressed in brightly colored robes leading an outdoor procession.

A painting of Ethiopia's most important saint, Maryam, or Mary

Other devotions include daily prayer and frequent fasting. Fasting means not eating any animal products, such as meat, eggs, or dairy foods. Wednesdays and Fridays are fasting days. People also fast for the several weeks leading up to Christmas and to Easter.

Saints and Holy Places

The most honored saint is Maryam—Mary, the mother of Jesus. Other important saints are Saint Gabriel, Saint Michael, and Saint George, the patron saint of Ethiopia.

There are also the so-called Nine Saints, who arrived around A.D. 480 from Syria. It is believed that they translated the Bible into Ge'ez and opened Ethiopia's first monasteries. Saints are depicted in many beautiful icons, or religious paintings, in Ethiopian Orthodox churches.

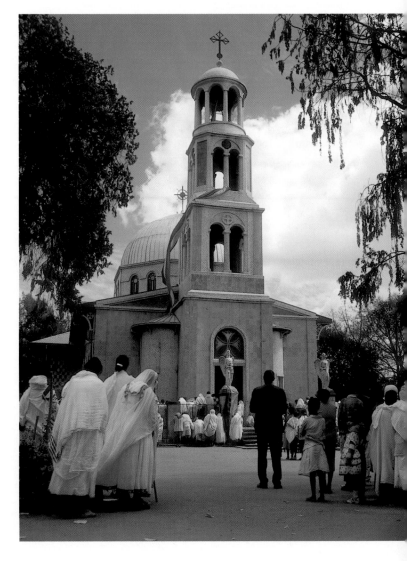

There are many churches throughout Ethiopia. This is Saint Mary's Church in Addis Ababa.

More than thirty thousand churches stand throughout the country. Most of them are round, but some may be rectangular or octagonal, having eight sides. Every church has three sections. The central part, behind a curtain, is the Holy of Holies, containing the tabot. Next is a section where people receive the Eucharist (Communion). The outer area of the church is the nave, where the congregation assembles. People must remove their shoes before entering.

Axum is the holiest city in the Ethiopian Orthodox Church. There, according to tradition, the Queen of Sheba reigned, and the Ark of the Covenant came to rest. Another religious center is Lalibela, with its famous churches hewn out of rock. Hundreds of priests and monks live in the city, and devout worshippers come for religious services. Lalibela is also a major pilgrimage site. Tens of thousands of people make the journey there to celebrate important feast days.

The Work of Angels?

Lalibela's stone churches were built within a rather short time. According to legend, stonecutters worked at their task all day. Then angels took over the hammering and chiseling, laboring all through the night.

Four of the eleven churches are enormous. Workers may have carved them starting at the top and working down to the floors, or they may have carved an open area around a rock and chiseled in from floor level. Visitors move among the churches through a maze of rock-enclosed alleys and tunnels.

The grandest of all the churches is Beta Medhane Alem (House of the World's Redeemer) (below). It measures 110 feet (33.5 m) long, 77 feet (23.5 m) wide, and 36 feet (11 m) high and has five naves, or large worship areas. Beta Maryam (House of Saint Mary) is noted for its walls and ceilings covered with paintings of animals and biblical scenes.

All eleven buildings are World Heritage sites, protected by the United Nations Educational, Scientific, and Cultural Organization (UNESCO).

Priests administer a symbolic baptism during Timkat.

Celebrations

Dozens of feast days are celebrated throughout the year. Every local church honors its patron saint's feast day, and people celebrate their personal saints' days, too. In addition, each day of every month is devoted to a certain saint. For example, the twelfth is devoted to Saint Michael, the nineteenth to Saint Gabriel, and the twenty-first to Saint Mary.

Timkat, on January 19, is a major religious holiday. It is called the feast of the Epiphany. In Western Christianity, the Epiphany celebrates the three wise men's visit to the infant Jesus. In Ethiopia, however, Timkat celebrates the baptism of Jesus. For the faithful it is a time to renew their faith through a symbolic baptism.

The night before Timkat, the tabot is removed from the church and housed in a tent beside a stream or sunken pool. People chant prayers there through the night. In the morning priests with colorful robes and tasseled umbrellas move in a solemn procession amid chanting, clapping, and beating drums. Arriving at the waterside, the priests bless the water and splash it onto the people.

The Feast of the True Cross, or Meskal, is celebrated every September with a torchlit procession.

Another great festival is Meskal, the Feast of the True Cross, on September 27. According to tradition, it celebrates the finding of the true cross on which Jesus was crucified. Saint Helena found the cross in Jerusalem by following the smoke from a fire. People celebrate Meskal by lighting a huge bonfire in their town square. They file in procession to the fire, carrying burning torches. Again, the celebrations last all through the night.

Islam Takes Root

Since its earliest days, Islam has had special ties to Ethiopia. Muhammad, called the Prophet, founded Islam in the seventh century A.D. He was born in Mecca, on the coast of present-day Saudi Arabia. Facing persecution, Muhammad sent his relatives and early followers to Axum for refuge. He knew they would be safe there because the Ethiopians were "godly people."

After the Prophet's death, Muslims swept through neighboring lands, converting vast regions to Islam. Axum, however, was considered off-limits. It was left untouched until at least the eighth century as a sign of gratitude for its protection of the first followers of the Prophet. Muslims are said to have established the city of Harer in the 700s. It later became a Muslim stronghold, with high walls for protection.

Gradually, Islam spread deeper into Ethiopia. At times both Muslim sultans and Christian kings ruled parts of the country at the same time. Deadly conflicts arose between the two religions, often over economic issues.

Today, however, people of both faiths live among one another peacefully. As religious conflicts flare up in other countries, Ethiopians are proud of their interfaith relations. Perhaps one reason for their peaceful coexistence is that both faiths incorporate elements of the same traditional culture and indigenous religions. Having lived side by side for centuries, they see each other as similar in spite of their differences.

The Walled City

The ancient walled city of Harer was a Muslim stronghold ruled by emirs, or Muslim princes. Harer thrived as an independent city for centuries, becoming a great center of trade and Islamic learning. Even today, Harer is considered one of the holy cities of Islam.

Most of Harer's city walls remain today, and visitors can enter through six huge gates. The Harer Gate is the main entrance. The city has about ninety mosques—the largest concentration of mosques in this small an area in the world. The emirs' palace is now a museum.

For many visitors Harer's "hyena man" is a fascinating attraction. Every night, he feeds hyenas outside the city walls. He gives them raw meat, holding it out on a stick. Eventually he gets bolder and holds the meat in his teeth for the hyenas to snatch.

Beliefs and Duties

Muslims believe in one God, whom they call Allah. Islam's holy scripture is the Qur'an (also spelled Koran). It contains the teachings of Muhammad and information about his life. The Qur'an is written in an early form of Arabic, the language of Muhammad. Muslims honor Moses, Abraham, Jesus, and many other religious figures as prophets. Muhammad is considered the last and greatest prophet of them all.

Traditionally, Muslims uphold the Five Pillars of Islam. The first is belief in Allah and his prophet Muhammad. The second is to pray at five set times during the day. During prayer a Muslim kneels and bows low, facing the holy city of Mecca. The third pillar is to fast during the holy month of Ramadan. This means abstaining from food, drink, and other pleasures from dawn to sunset. Giving aid to the poor is the fourth pillar. Finally, the fifth pillar is to make a pilgrimage to Mecca at least once in one's lifetime.

Public Religious Holidays

(O = Orthodox; M = Muslim)

O	Genna	Christmas	January 7
O	Timkat	Epiphany	January 19
M	'Id al-Adha	Abraham's sacrifice	Date varies
O	Good Friday	Death of Jesus	Spring (date varies)
O	Fasika	Easter	Spring (date varies)
M	Moulid	Birth of Muhammad	Date varies
O	Meskal	Feast of the True Cross	September 27
M	'Id al-Fitr	End of Ramadan	Date varies

While the Five Pillars are traditional duties, they are mostly observed by Muslims in the major cities. Villagers and nomadic people follow customs more suited to their lifestyles.

Mosques and Holy Days

Friday is Islam's holy day. On that day the faithful gather in the mosque, where an imam teaches and leads them in prayer. In Addis Ababa, the center of the Muslim community is Anwar Mosque. Its tall minarets, or towers, rise high over the

Anwar Mosque in Addis Ababa

Mercato. Brightly colored mosques are scattered throughout the countryside, too.

Muslims follow the Islamic calendar. It is a lunar calendar, following the cycles of the moon. Each year is about eleven days shorter than the western year. As a result, feast days fall on different days every year.

The most important Islamic holidays are 'Id al-Adha and 'Id al-Fitr. 'Id al-Adha celebrates the prophet Abraham's willingness to sacrifice his son. Families gather for a feast, sharing their food with not only friends and relatives but also the poor.

'Id al-Fitr comes at the end of Ramadan. With their month-long fast over, Muslims celebrate by feasting, giving gifts, and visiting one another. Moulid, the Prophet's birthday, is another important holiday.

The Falasha

In pre-Christian times a small community of Jews lived in Ethiopia. Various legends claim they were a lost tribe of Israelites or descendants of King Solomon. Eventually they settled in the north, around Lake Tana. They called themselves Beta Israel, or "House of Israel." Christian Ethiopians called them the Falasha. Their religious practices were a mixture of Jewish and Ethiopian traditions, with scriptures and ceremonies in the Ge'ez language.

In the early 1980s, the Falasha were devastated by civil war and drought. Israelis decided to help them immigrate to Israel, the Jewish homeland, under its law of return—the right of Jews worldwide to Israeli citizenship. In a series of dramatic

Ethiopian Jews, or Falasha, wait to be airlifted to Israel.

airlifts, thousands of Falasha refugees were transported to Israel. Between 1980 and 1992, more than forty thousand Falasha had emigrated. Today, only a few thousand Jewish people remain in Ethiopia. Most live in Addis Ababa.

Traditional Spirituality

Some of Ethiopia's tribal people honor traditional African deities. Several Oromo groups look to the sky god Waqa, whose eye is the sun. Waqa is the creator of all life and the

Ras Tafari

The name *ras*, meaning "head" in Amharic, was once a high military title for Ethiopian nobles. Haile Selassie's original name was Tafari Makonnen, so he was called Ras Tafari before becoming emperor.

In the 1950s, a movement called Rastafarianism arose among black people in Jamaica and other countries.

Its roots reached back even earlier, to the Back-to-Africa movement of the 1930s. Rastafarians looked to Haile Selassie as the Messiah and the religious and political savior of blacks. Some believers immigrated to Ethiopia, forming a Rastafarian community that exists to this day.

guardian of morality. The *ayana* are spirits who communicate between humans and Waqa. The *kallu* is a priest and intermediary. He may become possessed by the ayana to obtain blessings for the community.

Ancestors are important among many groups. The Konso memorialize their ancestors with *waga*, or tall posts that are carved with accounts of their deeds. This practice is declining, however, because so many waga are stolen by treasure hunters.

Good and evil spirits abound in Ethiopia's traditional religions. Good spirits may be appeased with prayers, ceremonies, or food offerings. The blessings people commonly seek are health, fertility, and rain. A priest may perform special rituals to drive out evil spirits that possess people or cause disease. Many groups make offerings to the spirits at holy places, such as sacred trees or rivers.

Even some Ethiopian Christians and Muslims believe in a variety of spirits. They may appeal to *zar* and *adbar* spirits for good harvests, protection from disease, and many other favors. Some people wear amulets, or charms, to ward off the evil eye. These beliefs, surviving from earlier times, are quickly dying out.

Many tribal groups worship only one god. His name may vary, but he is seen as the one supreme being. Traditional beliefs protect the social order, too. They preserve morality in personal life, family life, and community life. Many tribal people have converted to Christianity or Islam, yet still hold on to their old ways. It's sometimes said that converts wear their new religion like clothes over their traditional beliefs.

Living Traditions

I N ANY VILLAGE OR TOWN, CHILDREN CROWD AROUND VISITORS to sell their wares. They range from woolen rugs and hand-carved statues to decorated gourds and turtle-shell cowbells. Each ethnic group makes its own traditional handmade goods. These finely crafted items are made simply to meet the needs of everyday life.

Dorze weavers are known for their cotton textiles. They make their own traditional clothing items, including shawls with colorful borders. The Konso are known for weaving heavy cotton blankets. Rug making is a specialty in Debre Berhan, north of Addis Ababa. The woolen rugs feature simple patterns or the Lion of Judah design.

Opposite: **Beautifully crafted and handmade goods are meant to be used on a daily basis.**

Handwoven carpets have traditional patterns and designs.

Hareri women weave baskets using grasses that grow locally.

The Hareri and other people weave brightly colored baskets from native grasses. *Mesobs*, the biggest baskets, are used as tables for serving meals. The Falasha (Ethiopian Jews) are known for their red pottery figurines. Few Falasha are left, but people in the Gondar area still keep up this traditional craft.

Hardwood forests once flourished in Jimma, in western Ethiopia. Jimma artisans carved tree trunks into ornate three-legged stools and curved-back chairs. Carved wooden headrests are a specialty among some ethnic groups. These "pillows" preserve an elaborate hairstyle while the person sleeps.

With their abundance of cattle, Ethiopians make all kinds of leather goods, such as sandals, bags, and belts. The *agelgil* is a leather-covered basket. People in the highlands use it to carry food and supplies.

The Ethnological Museum

The Ethnological Museum in Addis Ababa explores the art and lifestyles of Ethiopia's many cultural groups. One section features clothing styles from different regions. Other sections show jewelry, weaving looms, furniture, huts, tools, coins, and medicinal charms. The art section displays religious art and ceremonial objects, including more than three hundred religious icons. Traditional musical instruments occupy another large section.

The museum is part of Addis Ababa University's Institute of Ethiopian Studies. It is housed in the former palace of Emperor Haile Selassie.

Fine Arts

Much of Ethiopia's fine art is related to the Ethiopian Orthodox Church. Walls and ceilings of many churches and monasteries are adorned with brilliantly colored religious scenes. Illuminated manuscripts are another type of religious art. They are handwritten copies of the Bible and other religious texts, beautifully illustrated with pictures and decorations.

Ethiopian crosses come in many intricate designs. Some are made of wood, while others are made of silver or gold and studded with jewels. They are displayed in churches and carried in processions. People have sometimes tried to smuggle these precious crosses out of the country. In a few cases they have succeeded. However, bags are now carefully checked for artifacts at Addis Ababa's airport.

The ceiling of Gondar's Debre Birhan Selassie church is an example of Ethiopia's religious art.

Modern artists in Ethiopia combine traditional art with current Western styles. Many artists paint traditional subjects on canvas, animal skins, and wood. Favorite subjects are King Solomon and the Queen of Sheba, Saint George and the dragon, and famous battles. Other recent paintings feature scenes from everyday life. Modern murals, or wall paintings, and stained-glass windows are seen, too. Addis Ababa's Africa Hall features dramatic stained-glass scenes by artist Afewerk Tekle.

Afewerk Tekle

Afewerk Tekle (1932–) is one of the best-known artists in Africa. Prints of his work hang in public buildings and homes all over Ethiopia. Besides canvas paintings, he creates drawings, murals, stained glass, and sculptures. His subjects range from landscapes and portraits to historical events and ancient cities. His most famous painting is *The Meskal Flower*.

Afewerk's monumental stained-glass windows adorn Addis Ababa's Africa Hall. The windows depict Africa in the past, present, and future. His art also is displayed in the capital's Saint George Cathedral. Afewerk has received dozens of international honors and awards for artistic excellence.

Looted Treasure

Ethiopians have seen many of their precious historic artifacts taken away. Among them is the Maqdala treasure. The treasure includes about five hundred religious manuscripts, as well as icons, gold and silver crosses, and two gold crowns. They were looted from Maqdala, the mountain fortress of Emperor Tewodros, in a British military campaign in 1868. The artifacts are now in the British Museum and other places. Ethiopia is pressuring the British government to return them.

Another precious item is the Axum Obelisk (left). This stone pillar, more than 80 feet (24 m) tall, is carved with door- and window-like openings. Erected in the second century A.D., it is one of Axum's largest and most ornate pillars. Italy's dictator Benito Mussolini had the obelisk carted away in 1937, erecting it in a square in Rome. The Italian government has now agreed to return the obelisk.

Ethiopians were outraged over the 1997 theft of an eight-hundred-year-old cross, the Afro Ayigeba. This large, richly decorated cross, believed to have healing power, was stolen from Lalibela's Beta Medhane Alem church. It was smuggled to Addis Ababa and sold to a Belgian antiques dealer, who sold it to a collector for $25,000. The collector returned the cross in 2001, and pilgrims continue to visit it.

Massinko player

Music, Song, and Dance

Ethiopian music is rousing, rhythmic, and full of life. Traditional instruments include the *krar*, a five- or six-stringed lyre that is strummed or plucked. The *massinko* is a one-stringed violin with a square sound box. *Azmari*, or wandering minstrels, used to play the massinko as they traveled with traders' caravans. The azmari still entertain people in Ethiopia's nightclubs.

The *negarit* is a huge drum that is beaten with sticks. When chiefs used to march through the countryside, their negarit players marched ahead of them. Each drum was strapped onto a donkey's back. The smaller *atamo* is a drum played with the hands. In the highlands, shepherd boys may play a reed flute called the *washint*. Its rippling tones are meant to calm the flocks.

Ethiopians enjoy a great variety of Amharic pop music. Many popular singers have fans who look for their latest tapes and CDs. Some musicians also play Ethiopian styles of jazz and blues. Western rock and rap music and Caribbean reggae enjoy a growing popularity among young people in urban areas such as Addis Ababa.

In rural areas, singing often accompanies farm chores and special occasions. Dancing is another way to celebrate and entertain. One dance may rejoice in the harvest, while another may act out a familiar legend. In the highlands the most popular traditional dance is the *iskista*. The dancers move their shoulders in a sharp rhythm, while their hips stay still.

Tribal Music Traditions

People in each ethnic group pass down their music traditions from one generation to the next. The Konso have a variety of songs they sing while performing farm chores and religious rituals and for entertainment. They play many handmade musical instruments, including flutes, lyres, bells, horns, and drums.

Jumping the Bulls

A Hamar boy must prove he is worthy of manhood. He does this in the *ukuli*—the jumping of the bulls. As many as thirty bulls are lined up side by side. The boy must leap onto the first bull, then run across the full length of the bulls' backs four times without falling off. If he succeeds, he has proved himself a worthy and capable man. He is welcomed into the *maz*—the name for adult men who are eligible for marriage.

Among the Hamar, singing is a favorite way to spend time together. Songfests can last for hours, stretching into the night. Women and girls sometimes play flutes as they guard the fields from hungry birds and baboons. Young men make the flutes from curled bark and cow dung. The Hamar also have songs to honor ancestors, call for war, and mourn the dead.

The Borana are famous for their "singing wells." Several people stand at different levels inside the well. As they pass up buckets of water, they sing a rhythmic song to keep pace with their moves.

The *fukara* is a boasting dance for young warriors or would-be warriors. The dancer holds a stick (or rifle) over his shoulders while shouting menacing threats. For some ethnic groups, dancing often involves vigorous leaping.

Religious Music

It is said that an Axumite musician named Yared introduced Ethiopian church music in the sixth century. He is credited with writing hundreds of hymns and inventing a way of writing down the musical notes. This system and his hymns are still used today. Yared was eventually declared a saint.

Music is an important part of Ethiopian Orthodox ceremonies. Each chant or hymn has its basic melody, and the singer improvises around it. Special instruments mark out the rhythm. One is a large drum called the *kebero*. It is made from a hollowed-out log with hides stretched around each end. Another is the *tsinatseil*, or *sistrum*. This elaborate rattle is said to have originated in ancient Egypt.

Religious processions bring out the most spectacular musical displays. All along the route people join in with singing, handclapping, drumbeating, and other joyous expressions. Sometimes a trumpet player leads the procession. Piercing the air is the high-pitched trill of women's traditional singing style.

Stories Great and Small

Ethiopia's national epic is the *Kebra Nagast* ("The Glory of Kings"). It tells the story of King Solomon and the Queen of Sheba, adding many rich details. The *Kebra Nagast* was written in the Ge'ez language in the 1300s.

Works of prose and poetry were often written in Ge'ez. Sadly, many of them were destroyed during the Muslim wars of the 1500s. In the 1850s and 1860s, Emperor Tewodros II directed the official narrative of his deeds to be written in Amharic. This helped make Amharic a respected language for literature as well as Ethiopia's official language.

Ethiopia is also rich in oral literature—wisdom passed on by word of mouth. Storytelling is a great form of entertainment to pass the time or finish off an evening meal. Many of Ethiopia's traditional folktales, fables, and proverbs (wise sayings) have been passed down for centuries. Their messages are clear because the characters have well-known reputations. They are often hyenas, jackals, lions, donkeys, and goats. Tales about animals such as crafty hyenas, mischievous monkeys, noble lions, and cunning snakes are used for teaching morality lessons to young children. Thus, animal tales have become part of the storytelling tradition.

Stroll down the road on a weekday afternoon and you may pass packs of young people all dressed alike. They might be wearing purple, blue, green, yellow, or some other bright color. They are students wearing their school uniforms, and most know how lucky they are to be in school.

Children in Ethiopia are required to attend school between ages seven and thirteen. However, only about 47 percent of primary-school-age children attend school. Of those who attend, there are more boys than girls. However, the number of girls in secondary and higher schools is growing fast.

Though all children aged seven to thirteen are supposed to attend school, fewer than half do.

There are many reasons why school attendance is so low. For one thing, much of Ethiopia's population lives in rural areas, where farming and herding are a way of life. Children's work is often vital to a family's survival. There are also fewer schools available in rural areas. Even in cities and towns, many children work instead of going to school. They may work as street peddlers, household servants, or shop helpers. The government is working to improve all these conditions, but the task is enormous.

Ethiopia offers free public schooling through grade ten. Primary school usually begins at age six or seven and lasts eight years. Secondary school comes in two cycles of two years each. After the first cycle, students take a national examination to see if they can move up to the next level. The second cycle prepares students to attend college or to perform technical jobs.

Ethiopia also has a system of traditional religious education. Many Ethiopian Orthodox churches have religious schools for boys, where they study church teachings, ceremonies, and scriptures. A boy may continue his religious studies if he hopes to become a priest or monk. Muslims also offer religious instruction for boys at mosques and madrasas (religious schools). This tradition is especially strong in Harer and other Muslim centers. Some other religious groups also have schools.

There are six universities and many more colleges in the country. Addis Ababa, the oldest and largest university, offers degrees in many subjects. The Alemaya University of Agriculture is near Harer, and the Medical College is in Gondar. Many junior colleges offer training in farming, technology, teaching, and other specialized subjects.

The Many Ways of Life

HOSPITALITY IS A WAY OF LIFE IN ETHIOPIA. EVEN PEOPLE who do not know English offer a cheerful "Hello!" or "Welcome!" to English-speaking visitors. Both friends and strangers get a friendly handshake from adults and children alike. Even in the bush—the country's remote, undeveloped areas—passing motorists get a smile and a wave.

Greetings are an important part of the culture in this friendly country. Relatives and friends may greet each other with three cheek kisses—right, left, and right. For many people greetings are a courteous ritual that may go on for some time. "How is your health, your family, your work, your harvest, your herd," and so on. The first order of business is checking on a person's well-being.

Opposite: **Daily life varies in Ethiopia depending on where a person lives.**

Round, thatched-roof homes outside the city of Harar

Cities and Towns

Daily life in Ethiopia is very different from one region to another. Cities, towns, and villages each have their distinctive sights, sounds, and ways of life. Addis Ababa has a pace of its own. Cars, trucks, and taxis weave around one another at sometimes frightening speeds.

Still, everyone seems to understand the rules of the road, and traffic accidents are rare.

Homes in the capital city range from apartment buildings to simple cottages to fine homes with courtyards and gardens. Toward the edges of town, sheep and goats graze by the roadside. Drifting through the air are smells of coffee, spices, incense, eucalyptus trees, and, at times, animal hides.

Outside the capital city, road travel takes on a different quality. Vehicles swerve around people and donkey carts carrying huge bundles of wood or crops. Sheep, goats, and cattle often share the same roads, so traffic stops as the animals slowly move aside. A lazy dog, a careless donkey, or a feasting vulture can hold up traffic, too.

Smaller cities are bustling with business, as a maze of traffic weaves among merchants and markets. Remote towns may have only one paved road. The side streets are dirt or gravel roads, all lined with tin-roofed homes and shops. Horse-and-buggy taxis (*garis*) trot through the streets, sometimes moving even faster than the cars.

Be Seven Years Younger!

"Visit Ethiopia and be seven years younger!" That's the promise of an Ethiopian tourism slogan. It is based on a fact of the Ethiopian calendar. Depending on the month, Ethiopia's years are seven or eight years behind the Gregorian (Western) calendar. For example, Ethiopia's year 1998 begins on September 11, 2005. (Ethiopia's New Year's Day is September 11.) The difference in years arises from the Ethiopian Orthodox Church's calculation of the date of the creation of the world.

Another slogan promises "thirteen months of sunshine!" This, too, is based on reality. Although it is said to follow the Julian calendar, Ethiopia breaks up the year as the Coptic calendar does—into thirteen months. Twelve months have thirty days each. The thirteenth month has five days, or six days in a leap year.

Life in the Countryside

In rural areas most people live as farmers or herders. Both adults and children go out every morning, sometimes traveling long distances, to graze their cattle and tend their fields. Plowing is done the centuries-old way, by a pair of yoked oxen pulling a wooden plow (*maresha*). Children often have the duty of guarding the fields. They perch on a high platform and throw stones at hungry baboons or birds that raid the crops.

Children keep animals away from the crops by standing atop platforms and slinging stones at them.

Across the countryside most houses are round. Their walls are clay-packed wood or bamboo poles, and their pointed roofs are thatched with grass. A clay pot on the rooftop covers a hole that lets smoke out. Inside, there is one area for cooking and another for sleeping. Each household may have a pen for livestock, a granary for storing grain, and cages for chickens. Newer homes are rectangular with tin roofs. In some regions people paint their homes with bright colors and intricate designs. Many towns in the north have stone houses surrounded by stone walls.

This woman in the countryside is proud of her brightly painted home.

Local farmers take their vegetables to the Harer marketplace.

Saturday is market day in many towns. People may walk for miles, often barefoot, carrying their goods to market. They are laden with enormous bundles of firewood, baskets of vegetables and fruits, or sacks of beans and grain. They take their places among merchants selling everything from plastic water jugs to donkeys and goats.

Everyday chores keep a steady pace to life, while special occasions add extra excitement. In Christian areas, churches are filled for the many festivals and saints' days. Among some ethnic groups there are birth, death, harvest, and coming-of-age ceremonies.

Nonreligious National Holidays

Enqutatash (New Year's Day)	September 11
Victory of Adwa Day	March 2
Patriots' Day (end of Italian occupation in 1941)	May 5
Downfall of the Derg	May 28

Clothing and Other Adornments

Clothing styles differ from one region to another. In cities and towns many residents wear Western-style clothes. In the northern highlands the *shamma* is the everyday dress for both men and women. It is a white cotton cloak worn over a cotton shirt or dress. Women's cotton dresses and shawls often have brightly colored borders.

Ethiopia's minority communities wear a colorful variety of clothing. Hamar, Tsamai, and Banna women wear animal skins decorated with cowrie shells, beads, and embroidery. Beaded belts and headbands complete the outfit. Men may wear only a simple cloak or a short cloth skirt. Clothing among the Borana is quite different. The men wear long robes, and women and girls wear dresses and scarves of bright green, blue, and yellow.

The white shamma is the everyday dress in northern cities and towns.

Above left: **A Karo tribesman**

Above right: **Hamar woman**

Armbands, necklaces, and earrings are important adornments. In many ethnic groups jewelry is a sign of a woman's status. It tells whether she is married or unmarried and whether she is a first wife. Women of the Mursi tribe wear a large clay plate in their lower lip. Karo women wear a nail or spike through the lower lip. The men often decorate their entire bodies in white paint made from ash.

In many regions women wear their hair in tiny cornrows. Hamar women wear neat braids or ringlets rubbed with ocher to give them a reddish tint. The men may wear elaborate hairdos with a clay base that anchors ostrich feathers.

He Endures!

Haile Gebreselassie is one of the greatest long-distance runners of all time. Born in 1973 in Arsi Province, Haile was one of nine children. Every day, he would run 6 miles (10 km) to school and back. It was great preparation for his future as a champion runner. By 2004, Haile had set eighteen world records. Among his proudest victories are his two Olympic gold medals. He won the gold in the 10,000-meter race in the 1996 and 2000 Olympic Games. Haile starred as himself in the 1999 movie *Endurance*.

Land of Champs

Football—which Americans call soccer—is the most popular sport in Ethiopia. From big cities to remote towns, it is a common sight to see kids kicking a soccer ball through the streets. The national team plays in the National Stadium in Addis Ababa. Many offices and factories have their own soccer teams, too.

Ethiopia has produced many great athletes, especially in long-distance running events. The legendary runners Abebe Bikila, Mamo Wolde, and Miruts Yifter are national heroes. Abebe became world-famous when he won the marathon event in the 1960 Olympics—running in bare feet! He won the gold once again in the 1964 Olympics. Mamo took the gold in the 1968 Olympic marathon, and Miruts captured two gold medals in the 1980 games. The reigning champ today is Haile Gebreselassie (see sidebar above).

Ethiopia's female runners are just as impressive. In 1992, Derartu Tulu became the first African woman ever to win an

Playing *Gebata*

Gebata is a board game played in Ethiopia and many other African countries. This ancient game has many regional variations. It is played on a long board with two rows of six holes each. At each end is a large hole. To begin, two players face each other across the board. In each small hole are four pebbles, beads, or tiny balls. Each player moves the pebbles, trying to capture the other's pieces and get as many as possible into the hole on the end.

Olympic gold medal. Her victory lap after the 10,000-meter race, draped in the national flag, was an unforgettable sight. Fatuma Roba continued the Olympic tradition when she won the women's marathon in 1996.

Food and Drink

Ethiopia's national food is injera. This flatbread looks like a huge pancake. Ethiopians eat it with almost everything. Injera is not only a bread—it is also a serving plate. Mounds of delicious foods are served on top of it. Another type of bread is made from ensete (false banana). The dough is shaped into a round, flat loaf and cooked over a fire.

The most popular meat dish is *wot*, a spicy stew of lamb, beef, chicken, or beans. Tilapia and Nile perch are some of the

Making Injera

To make injera, a cook mixes teff flour with water to make a batter. The batter is left to stand and ferment for about three days. Then it is poured from a pitcher onto a round clay baking sheet over a fire. Soon bubbles rise up to cover the surface. The cook slides the baked bread off the fire and onto a serving platter. Then mounds of delicious foods are placed on top—spicy meat, lentils, beans, cabbage, and other vegetables.

Eating injera is an art in itself. With the right hand, tear off a piece of bread. Lay it over a mound of food and pinch to make a tight little sandwich. Then eat and enjoy!

The Bunna Ceremony

To begin the bunna ceremony, the hostess spreads green branches and flowers around the serving area. She lights one fire to perfume the air with incense and another to roast the coffee beans. Next, she grinds the roasted beans to a powder, adds it to a coffeepot (*jebena*), and sets the pot over burning coals. Meanwhile, she arranges several tiny cups (*sini*) on a platter.

When the coffee is ready, she fills each cup and passes it to a guest. This cup, from the first brewing, is the strongest. The second and third cups that are brewed are weaker. It is polite for a guest to stay for all three cups. For people who are always in a hurry, it is a reminder to slow down and take time to enjoy good friends and conversation.

tasty fish from Ethiopia's lakes and streams. Spicy vegetable dishes are substituted for meats on fasting days.

Ethiopians enjoy a variety of freshly picked ripe fruits. Pineapples, papayas, mangoes, bananas, and oranges are just a few. Other fresh foods include potatoes, cabbage, carrots, tomatoes, spinach, peas, beans, onions, and hot peppers. The peppers add a spicy flair to many dishes.

Coffee and tea are favorite drinks, as well as soft drinks, beer, and *tej* (honey wine). Coffee is served as a sign of friendship and goodwill. Guests in both restaurants and private homes are welcomed with the *bunna* (coffee) ceremony. It's an old tradition in Ethiopia's culture—and a perfect expression of the warmth and hospitality of these kind and gracious people.

Timeline

Ethiopian History

People speaking Omotic and Cushitic languages live in Ethiopia's highlands.	**c. 7000** B.C.
Ethiopians trade with Egypt.	**c. 3000** B.C.
People begin migrating to Ethiopia from Saba (present-day Yemen) on the Arabian Peninsula, bringing their Sabaean writing system, which develops into Ethiopia's Ge'ez script.	**c. 1000** B.C.
The Axumite kingdom rises in the northern highlands.	**c. 200** B.C.
Axumite king Ezana converts to Christianity and makes it Ethiopia's official religion.	**c. A.D. 330**
Muslim Arabs begin taking over Axum's trade along the Red Sea.	**Early 700s**
Zagwe dynasty rules Ethiopia.	**c.1137–1270**
Zagwe king Lalibela has eleven churches carved out of solid rock.	**Early 1200s**
Amharic prince Yekuno Amlak restores the Solomonid dynasty.	**1270**
Muslim leader Ahmad Grañ begins a military conquest of Ethiopia.	**c. 1520**
Emperor Fasilidas comes to power, establishing his capital at Gondar.	**1632**

World History

2500 B.C.	Egyptians build the Pyramids and the Sphinx in Giza.
563 B.C.	The Buddha is born in India.
A.D. 313	The Roman emperor Constantine recognizes Christianity.
610	The Prophet Muhammad begins preaching a new religion called Islam.
1054	The Eastern (Orthodox) and Western (Roman) Churches break apart.
1066	William the Conqueror defeats the English in the Battle of Hastings.
1095	Pope Urban II proclaims the First Crusade.
1215	King John seals the Magna Carta.
1300s	The Renaissance begins in Italy.
1347	The Black Death sweeps through Europe.
1453	Ottoman Turks capture Constantinople, conquering the Byzantine Empire.
1492	Columbus arrives in North America.
1500s	The Reformation leads to the birth of Protestantism.

Ethiopian History

Menelik II becomes emperor.	**1889**
Ethiopian army defeats invading Italians at the Battle of Adwa.	**1896**
Emperor Haile Selassie I comes to power.	**1930**
Italian forces occupy Ethiopia.	**1936–1941**
Mengistu Haile Mariam leads a military takeover; a committee called the Derg establishes a socialist state; anthropologists in the Hadar region discover a female skeleton that is more than 3 million years old and name her Lucy.	**1974**
Drought causes the worst famine in Ethiopia's history.	**1984–1985**
The Ethiopian People's Revolutionary Democratic Front (EPRDF) topples the Derg regime.	**1991**
Eritrea becomes independent.	**1993**
Ethiopia adopts a constitution.	**1994**
Ethiopia holds its first multiparty elections.	**1995**
Border war with Eritrea ends in a peace treaty.	**2000**
Anthropologists in the Hadar region discover the remains of human ancestors that are more than 5 million years old.	**2001**

World History

1776	The Declaration of Independence is signed.
1789	The French Revolution begins.
1865	The American Civil War ends.
1914	World War I breaks out.
1917	The Bolshevik Revolution brings communism to Russia.
1929	Worldwide economic depression begins.
1939	World War II begins, following the German invasion of Poland.
1945	World War II ends.
1957	The Vietnam War starts.
1969	Humans land on the moon.
1975	The Vietnam War ends.
1979	Soviet Union invades Afghanistan.
1983	Drought and famine in Africa.
1989	The Berlin Wall is torn down, as communism crumbles in Eastern Europe.
1991	Soviet Union breaks into separate states.
1992	Bill Clinton is elected U.S. president.
2000	George W. Bush is elected U.S. president.
2001	Terrorists attack World Trade Towers, New York and the Pentagon, Washington, D.C.
2003	A coalition of forty-nine nations, headed by the United States and Great Britain, invade Iraq.

Fast Facts

Official name: Federal Democratic Republic of Ethiopia

Capital: Addis Ababa

Official language: Amharic

Other languages: Oromifa, Tigrinya, Guaraginga, Somali, other local languages, English

Thatched-roof homes outside Harar

Ethiopia's flag

The landscape

National anthem:	"Whedefit Gesgeshi Woude Henate Ethiopia" ("March Forward, Dear Mother Ethiopia"); adopted in 1992
Government:	Federal republic
Chief executive:	Prime minister
Head of state:	President
Area:	435,184 square miles (1,127,127 sq km)
Borders:	Eritrea to the north and northeast; Djibouti and Somalia to the east, Kenya to the south; Sudan to the west
Highest elevation:	Ras Dejen, 15,158 feet (4,620 m) above sea level
Lowest elevation:	Danakil Depression, 410 feet (125 m) below sea level
Greatest distance north to south:	800 miles (1,287 km)
Greatest distance east to west:	1,035 miles (1,665 km)
Largest lake:	Lake Tana, about 1,400 square miles (3,626 sq km)
Major rivers:	Blue Nile (Abay), Omo, Awash, and Wabe Shebele
Average temperatures:	Highlands: 62°F (17°C); lowlands: 82°F (28°C)
Highest annual rainfall:	Up to 80 inches (203 cm) in the southwestern highlands
Lowest annual rainfall:	0–20 inches (0–51 cm) in the Danakil Plain
National population (2004 est.):	72,035,400

Axum obelisk

Population of largest cities (2004 est):

Addis Ababa	2,763,500
Dire Dawa	254,500
Nazret	176,800
Gondar	147,900
Mekele	133,500
Bahir Dar	131,800

Famous landmarks:

- ▶ *Ark of the Covenant chapel, Saint Mary of Zion Church*, Axum
- ▶ *Church of Saint Mary*, Mount Entoto
- ▶ *Blue Nile Falls*, near Bahir Dar
- ▶ *Debre Damo monastery*, northeast of Axum
- ▶ *Fasilidas's palace complex*, Gondar
- ▶ *Lake Tana monasteries*, islands and shores of Lake Tana
- ▶ *Menelik's Palace*, Addis Ababa
- ▶ *Palace of Aba Jifar*, Jimma
- ▶ *Rock-hewn churches*, Lalibela
- ▶ *Stelae Park*, Axum
- ▶ *Walled Muslim city*, Harer

Industry: Agriculture is Ethiopia's major industry. Coffee is the most important export crop, and teff is the leading crop for domestic use. Leather goods, cotton textiles, and processed foods are some of the major manufactured goods. Gold, limestone, and marble are important minerals.

Currency

Currency: The birr is Ethiopia's basic unit of currency. In November 2004, US$1.00 was equal to 8.434 birr, and 1 birr was equal to US$0.119.

System of weights and measures: The metric system is Ethiopia's official system of weights and measures.

Schoolchildren

Literacy rate (2003 est.):	42.7% (male, 50.3%; female, 35.1%)	

Common Amharic Words and Phrases:

Selam (seh-LAHM)	Hello (peace be with you)
Tenastilign/tenastelen (teh-NAH-steh-lehn)	Hello (may you have good health)
Denaneh?/denanesh? (deh-NAH-neh/ deh-NAH-nesh)	How are you? (to a man/woman)
Dehna nenyi (DEH-nah NEHN-yee)	I'm fine
Dehna hun/hunyi (DEH-nah HOON/ HOON-yee)	Good-bye (to a man/woman)
Ow (OW)	Yes
Aye or aydelem (EYE or EYE-deh-lehm)	No
Amesegenalew (ah-meh-seh-geh-NAH-lew)	Thank you

Haile Selassie I

Famous Ethiopians:

Ezana (A.D. fourth century)
Axumite king who adopted Christianity

Fasilidas (reigned 1632–1667)
Emperor who established Gondar as Ethiopia's capital

Haile Selassie I (1892–1975)
Ethiopia's last emperor (reigned 1930–1974)

Lalibela (?–1225)
Emperor who had churches carved out of rock in the city of Lalibela

Menelik II (1844–1913)
Emperor who unified and modernized Ethiopia

Tewodros II (reigned c. 1818–1868)
Emperor who reunified Ethiopia and began the modernization process

Yekuno Amlak (?–1285)
Emperor who restored the Solomonid dynasty

To Find Out More

Nonfiction

▶ Berg, Elizabeth. *Ethiopia*. Milwaukee: Gareth Stevens, 2000.

▶ Fanouris, Mellina and Lukas Fanouris. *Meskel: An Ethiopian Family Saga, 1926–1981*. Nairobi, Kenya: Jacaranda Designs, 1995.

▶ Grunsell, Angela. *Ethiopia*. Crystal Lake, IL: Rigby Interactive Library, 1996.

▶ Lassieur, Allison. *Ethiopia*. Mankato, MN: Capstone, 2003.

▶ Marsh, Richard. *Black Angels: The Art and Spirituality of Ethiopia*. Oxford, UK.: Lion Publishing, 2001.

▶ Mezlekia, Nega. *Notes from the Hyena's Belly: An Ethiopian Boyhood*. New York: Picador USA, 2002.

▶ Peffer, John. *States of Ethiopia*. New York: Franklin Watts, 1998.

▶ Waterlow, Julia. *A Family from Ethiopia*. Austin: Raintree/Steck-Vaughn, 1998.

▶ Zuehlke, Jeffrey. *Ethiopia in Pictures*. Minneapolis: Lerner, 2004.

Fiction

▶ Ashabranner, Brent, Russell Davis, and Helen Siegl (illustrator). *The Lion's Whiskers and Other Ethiopian Tales*. North Haven, CT: Linnet Books, 1997.

▶ Kurtz, Jane, and Jean-Paul Tibbles (illustrator). *Saba: Under the Hyena's Foot*. Middleton, WI: Pleasant Company Publications, 2003.

▶ Laird, Elizabeth. *When the World Began: Stories Collected from Ethiopia*. New York: Oxford University Press, 2000.

▶ Mezlekia, Nega. *The God Who Begat a Jackal*. New York: Picador USA, 2003.

Videotapes

▶ *Endurance*. Disney Studios, 2003. 83 minutes.

▶ *Ethiopia*. Lonely Planet, 1999.

▶ *Ethiopia: The Kingdom of Judas Lion*. NY: Ambrose Video, 1998. 27 minutes.

▶ *The Kwegu*. London: Royal Anthropological Institute, 1982. 50 minutes.

▶ *The Migrants*. London: Royal Anthropological Institute, 1985. 52 minutes.

▶ *Mountains of Faith*. Washington, D.C.: National Geographic, 2001. 60 minutes.

▶ *The Mursi*. London: Royal Anthropological Institute, 1974. 52 minutes.

Web Sites

▶ **Selamta**
http://www.selamta.net/index.htm
An exploration of Ethiopia's people, culture, history, wildlife, and interesting sites.

▶ **Ethiopian Embassy**
http://www.ethioembassy.org.uk/
Lots of information on Ethiopia, including government, sports, and national parks.

▶ **Ethioworld**
http://www.ethioworld.com/Country Information/countryinformation.htm
Information on Ethiopia's land, history, religion, arts, calendar, and much more.

Embassy

▶ **Embassy of Ethiopia**
3506 International Drive N.W.
Washington, D.C. 20008
202-364-1200

Index

Page numbers in *italics* indicate illustrations.

Gurage, 79
Omo Valley tribes, 81, *81*
Oromo, 78, *78*
Sidama, 79
Somalis, 80
Tigrean, 79
Piazza, 62, *62*
plant life, 34–36
poachers/poaching, 31
political parties, 52, 61
population
density map, *78*
ethnic provinces, *79*
major cities, *81*
national, 77
Portugal/Portuguese, 45, 47
Ptolemy Dynasty, 41

R

radio, 75
Rastafarianism, 104
rebels at Presidential Palace, *53*
refugees during famine, *52*
regions and provinces, *23*
religion
Ark of the Covenant, 46, 92, 93
Christianity, 43
Islam, 43, 99, 101–103
Judaism (Falasha), 103–104, *104*
monasteries, 89–91
Orthodox Church, 43, 47, 87–89,
93–94
pilgrimage sites, 16
Roman Catholicism, 47
traditional spirituality, 104–105
see also churches

religious
art, 109, *109*
battles and power struggles, 47
devotions, Orthodox, 93–94
diversity, 87
holidays and celebrations, 34,
97–99, 101
holy days, Muslim, 102–103
music, 114–115
saints and holy places, 94–96
schools, 117
text and pictures, *43*
rivers, *20*, 20–21

S

Sahle Miriam. *See* Menelik II
Saint Mary's Church, 95
salt workers, *71*
savannah trees, 36
schoolchildren, *116*
service industry, 69–70
Shabele River, 20
Sheba, Queen of, 46, *46*
Simien Mountains, 16, *17*
Simien Mountains National Park,
33–34, *34*
slavery, 50
Solomonid Dynasty, 41, 44–45
Solomon Lulu Mitiku, 59
Somalis, 51–52
Soviet Union, 52
Spain, 47
sports, 125–126
stone pillars in Axum, *25*, *42*
storytelling, 115
Susenyos (emperor), 47

Meet the Author

ANN HEINRICHS fell in love with faraway places while reading Doctor Dolittle books as a child. Now she tries to cover as much of the Earth as possible. She has traveled through most of the United States and much of Europe, as well as the Middle East, East Asia, and Africa. In Ethiopia she enjoyed getting to know the tribal people of the Omo Valley, trekking through the countryside, chasing baboons and warthogs, exploring ancient churches and monasteries, and devouring injera. The photo at right shows Ann and a Konso girl in a schoolyard in Filwha.

Ann grew up roaming the woods of Arkansas. Now she lives in Chicago. She is the author of more than one hundred books for children and young adults on American, European, Asian, and African history and culture.

"To me, writing nonfiction is a bigger challenge than writing fiction. With nonfiction, you can't just dream something up—everything has to be true. Finding out facts is harder than making things up, but to me it's more rewarding. When I

uncover the facts, they always turn out to be more spectacular than fiction. And I'm always on the lookout for what kids in another country are up to, so I can report back to kids here."

Ann has also written numerous newspaper, magazine, and encyclopedia articles. As an advertising copywriter, she has covered everything from plumbing hardware to Oriental rugs. She holds bachelor's and master's degrees in piano performance. More recently, her performing arts have been tai chi empty-hand and sword forms. She is an award-winning martial artist and participates in regional and national tournaments.

Photo Credits

Photographs © 2005:

3 2186 00147 1886